Dark Goddesses

Unlocking the Power of Hecate, Lilith, The Morrigan, Baba Yaga, Kali, Oya, Persephone, Hathor, Sekhmet, and More

Your Free Gift
(only available for a limited time)

Thanks for getting this book! If you want to learn more about various spirituality topics, then join Mari Silva's community and get a free guided meditation MP3 for awakening your third eye. This guided meditation mp3 is designed to open and strengthen ones third eye so you can experience a higher state of consciousness. Simply visit the link below the image to get started.

https://spiritualityspot.com/meditation

Or, Scan the QR code!

Table of Contents

Introduction

Feared by many and venerated by others, and with their origins, roles, and true powers often shrouded in mystery, the Dark Goddesses are unique representations of negative forces in different cultures. Every culture had them in its pantheon, and, in some, they were even more respected than the benevolent deities because no one dared to anger them. This book explores the archetype of these Dark Goddesses, unveiling what made them so powerful and significant for ancient and modern followers alike. You will learn how they're tied to Jung's theory of the shadow self and how this might lead to the exploration of one's inner Dark Goddess.

This book presents a multilayered insight into the roles and attributes of Greek, Egyptian, Mesopotamian, Slavic, Hindu, African, Celtic, and Norse Dark Goddesses. Unlike other books in its category, which only focus on the mythological aspects of these deities, this book also explores their history and spiritual significance for modern spiritual seekers. Whether you are just dipping your toes into spiritual practices or have some experience in shadow work, goddess worship, neo-paganism, and other alternative practices, this book will empower you to unlock the transformative potential and inner wisdom Dark Goddesses embody.

The book relays theoretical and practical information in a beginner-friendly, easily-to-grasp way, making it easier for everyone to relate to and enrich their spiritual journey. Whether you're open to exploring different spiritual paths and looking to embrace a diverse range of spiritual traditions or wish to learn about the dark deities from a specific culture, this book will be the perfect stepping stone for your new adventures.

If you relate to the divine feminine and are seeking knowledge and inspiration from powerful female deities, this guide will show you how to obtain it all from the right sources. Through a profound and esoteric exploration of the darker sides of the goddesses, this book will teach you how to acknowledge the complexity of their symbolism, myths, and, most importantly, the vast empowerment they can bestow on you. If you are ready to expand your spiritual wisdom through a profound understanding and embracing female divine energies, don't hesitate to read on.

Chapter 1: The Archetype of the Dark Goddess

To help you understand the origins, symbolism, and meaning of the term "Dark Goddess," this chapter explores the concept of darkness in multifaceted contexts of spirituality, psychology, and mythology in a range of cultures and spiritual traditions. After introducing the book's central theme and the significance of transformation through the darkness and shadow, this chapter outlines a deeper perspective, including primary and esoteric information about the Dark Goddess archetype.

The Concept of the Dark Goddess

The concept of Dark Goddesses is based on an archetype representing similar roles, attributes, and functions in different cultures. Esoterically speaking, the archetype is defined as a causal presence of a causal energy or one that lives in the causal part of the spirit, known as the *psyche*. It is created (naturally through thoughts or magical acts) in the psyche, and it can die there, too, if its energy ceases to exist. This indicates that the Dark Goddess archetype is a living being that only manifests in people's psyche. Once created, the archetype continues to be present in the causal continuum, meaning it affects people's lives because they believe in it.

These female deities became associated with war and destruction.
https://pixabay.com/photos/woman-angel-raven-dark-fashion-8171684/

As the New Age pagan and other alternative religions gained popularity, the idea of these powerful dark beings grew alongside this renewed interest. The reason behind this was simple. While often misunderstood, Dark Goddesses are the ultimate representation of authenticity and diversity. Working with a Dark Goddess enables you to shine a light on these topics - and many others that are repressed by modern society. Because they may be pushed aside, they remain lurking in the shadows, just like dark female deities do in legends. They can guide the practitioner toward healing, which is often seen as rebirth as it frees them from societal expectations and other burdens that obstruct their authenticity. Due to its prominent energy, the archetype is a true powerhouse, capable of rewriting the narratives of the lives of those seeking freedom and empowerment through the divine feminine.

As an archetype, the Dark Goddess is only one facet of a female deity. Many turn to work with ancient goddesses because they promise brightness and positivity. However, sometimes, life forces you to explore the goddess's other side because they often hold answers to negative experiences, thoughts, and emotions. In fact, the deities identified with this archetype are only called Dark Goddesses because of their controversial portrayal by certain cultures who didn't understand their roles and origins. In cultures where patriarchal views were prevalent, these female deities became associated with war and destruction, with many a patriarch claiming they had an unusual desire to spill blood. By contrast, in cultures that embrace and honor dark female energies, the Dark Goddess is seen as part of a whole, the part that deals with frightening and troublesome yet necessary experiences of life. While the lighter sides nurture, heal, and protect, the darker ones teach how to fight, confront your enemies (both physically and metaphorically), and overcome the most formidable obstacles in life. In many legends and stories, the Dark Goddesses were summoned to chase away true evil and purify the space/person/object it inhabited.

Jungian Analysis and the Shadow Self

Mysterious, destructive, chaotic, associated with the occult - the Dark Goddess archetype is all that. However, it is also transformational as it provides a holistic insight into oneself and nature. The nature of these female deities is also dark, which, on one hand, is indicative of the female empowerment experience. On the other hand, this nature is the perfect embodiment of what renowned psychologist Carl Jung called the "shadow self."

In multiple religions, the Dark Goddess archetype is the part of nature that should be avoided or prevented from flourishing. Despite differences in their backstories, Dark Goddesses in Eastern and Western cultures were viewed similarly. One of the key differences was that in Western cultures, the archetype was seen as the projection of patriarchy, hence the association with hostile intentions and warfare.

When referring to human nature, darkness was also something people were encouraged to stay away from. While it's easy to see why one would want to discourage people from approaching and embracing one's darkest self, repressing it is also not recommended because it prevents them from understanding their true nature, values, and spiritual needs. Since this is a much-debated topic in religious communities and among alternative practitioners, understanding the archetype's significance for personal empowerment requires a deeper exploration. This is where delving into Jung's psychodynamics and theoretical analysis of the human psyche comes in handy.

While Gustav Jung was primarily concerned about the human psyche, he and his students also thoroughly researched the goddess concept, effectively drawing a line between psychoanalysis and esoteric practices. Jung named the goddess anime, or animal mundi (which translates as world soul), implicating not only that people live in a goddess-centered world but that the goddess lives within everyone.

According to Jung, the Dark Goddess archetype is the manifestation of the "shadow self," standing in opposition to the "ego self." The self represents the entirety of the psyche, combining the subconscious and conscious parts. As the most authentic core of one's being, the self gives way to traits and characters, including the persona and the anima/animus; the latter are gendered parts of the collective subconscious. The anima is how the male psyche envisions the feminine, and the animus is how the female psyche infers the male one. The persona is the part of yourself you convey to the world.

Jung saw the ego as the core and main driver of one's persona - the part everyone is conscious of and controls through their actions. However, Jung considered that there must be a balance to the ego, partially because while treating patients, he discovered that deep down, people are always aware of their true nature and personality even if they don't show this awareness to the outside world. He called this hidden part "the shadow" and argued that reaching it requires immense effort. However, by raising awareness of one's shadow self, you can identify the darkest aspects of your personality and acknowledge them as real parts of your existence. For most people, this goes against their every core belief, so they'll naturally resist conceding to their shadow self. The main reason for resistance can be found in the patriarchal theological concept of evil, which dictates that the dark part of oneself is bad and, therefore, must be repressed.

Jung called the process of raising self-awareness of one's complex nature Individuation. According to him, facing one's shadow is the first step on this journey. Instead of viewing the dark side as something to be ashamed of, Jung encouraged people to confront the part of themselves that prompts them to do evil things. He claimed that since these are natural parts of everyone's personality, it's better to get to know them closely rather than to avoid it as if it would lead to a road of corruption. He considered that seeing the shadow as inherently flawed can do more harm to your psyche than embracing it and trying to work with it.

Jung's theory about the Dark Goddess archetype being the epitome of the shadow self offers a fantastic way to describe and experience internalized experiences. What's ineffable to some people, followers of Dark Goddesses can embrace it as a natural experience without any biases, doubt, or questions. Regardless of what your beliefs are, the goddess teaches you about the importance of experience, effectively validating the things you can't explain through rational thoughts and concepts.

Jung's theories provide an empowering and genuine intrinsic source of power in the Dark Goddess. Whether it was through identifying her as an individual female divinity in a vast pantheon of deities or seeing her as the face of a multi-faceted goddess, this is exactly how the archetype is portrayed in several religions. Buttressing Jung's claims of how much effort it requires to face the darkness within, many tales describe the high price paid by those approaching the goddess. Known to bring people to the edge of extreme psychological exhaustion, these dark female forces demand a great deal. You cannot simply hope for the best when encountering these deities, which is why interaction with them is ill-advised unless you are truly prepared to handle their power.

On more than one occasion, practitioners describe experiencing a significant negative shift when calling on a Dark Goddess. Considering Jung's theories, this is to be expected. After all, confronting one's dark self also brings up many negative emotions, including fear, helplessness, anxiety, and weakness. Yet, without experiencing these, you cannot learn your own strength. If you never face anything that upsets or scares you, how do you know you'll have the courage to overcome it? Only by confronting your weaknesses can you ever understand what it takes to summon your strength. It's a powerful but much-needed lesson the archetype teaches. The goddesses also show that just as everyone can be compassionate and loving when empowered, their power can also come from anger, pain, and other negative emotions and experiences (and use it for great purposes).

While facing your dark self often results in the destruction of previous beliefs, this is necessary to rebuild yourself. Before working with the Dark Goddess, you're only living driven by the conscious part of yourself. Afterward, you become whole and find your individual strength. This is where the true power of the Dark Goddess archetype lies.

Over time, Jung's theories that tied the archetype to a person's personality and psyche became widely accepted. Some were purely intrigued by this mysterious power, while others realized the importance of further exploration of this highly neglected archetype. Interestingly enough, Jung viewed the Dark Goddess both as a female shadow self (anima) and the dark aspect of the male shadow (animus). The latter explains why so many people don't want to concede to this aspect within their psyche. It goes against the male ego, which doesn't like to think it has weaknesses, fears, and insecurities. However, its shadow knows it does, and contrary to other popular beliefs, it's not evil or negative either. The female shadow empowers the person to acknowledge this part of their psyche, weaknesses, faults, and all.

The multitude of Dark Goddesses you can work with have their own particular powers. By summoning the ones you identify with or truly need, you can find the way forward in your empowerment journey. For example, by calling on a goddess symbolizing freedom and lust, you can learn to suppress your guilt about not following societal expectations blindly (virtually no one does because it's impossible given how many there are and how baffling they can be). Likewise, by summoning a goddess of transformation, you can heal from past traumas and use them instead to illustrate growth.

Those following in Jung's footsteps helped transform the goddess from a simple archetype into a full-blown movement. They brought the archetype alive from the causal psyche and into the real world, proving its existence. This helped popularize the concept of the divine feminine, both in its own transcendent nature (which helps identify it in oneself) and as the driving force behind new and re-emerging religions that worship Dark Goddesses as transcendent divine beings.

Dark Goddess Archetype Representations

In many cultures, the Dark Goddess is seen as a sinister female creature with origins in ancient traditions, much older than the myths of their benevolent counterparts. Known as the Mother of Blood and Mistress of Destruction, among others, this archetype's contemporary definition is often tied to how these female deities are represented in popular religions and traditions. These often illustrate dark female deities as beautiful women in their prime, wearing provocative clothing or even having a naked form. They also claim that in ancient times, these goddesses could only be appeased via human sacrifices and were never to be addressed by their names.

Yet, in the same vein, these representations empower women beyond the ways they are depicted in their benevolent, nurturing goddess form. While it's true that this empowerment comes from the divine female's sinister ability to dabble in the occult, it can't be denied that they play vital roles in people's lives, evolution, and collective growth. Female empowerment may be hidden behind esoteric concepts and mysterious and misunderstood pagan practices, yet it's clear that women can obtain it by working on themselves and developing their ability to control their entire self.

Unlike some pagan and Wiccan practitioners who see the divine feminine as a calm, serene, yet independent ethos, the depiction of the Dark Goddess archetype isn't afraid to highlight the dark feminine principle. Women don't have to adopt a male behavior to be as powerful as men are. They can find the empowerment within to feel, behave, and grow to be equal to men. At the same time, the archetype teaches men that acknowledging their weaknesses won't make them appear feminine. Followers of Dark Goddesses learn that both genders have much more to offer than those qualities traditionally ascribed to them. Despite their best intention of not harming anyone, no one embodies this "perfect" quality. It's not possible to never make a mistake or hurt anyone. *If nothing else, you'll eventually hurt yourself.*

It's not uncommon for Dark Goddesses to be shown as opportunistic and vengeful, especially when it comes to punishing mortals. Yet, true followers know that while they are easily angered, the wrath of a Dark Goddess is never undeserved or without a cause. Some people just need a bigger push (or a powerful lesson) to embrace and understand their relation to themselves and every other being in the universe. Albeit in an unusual way, the goddesses teach empathy for everything and everyone around you, as well as for yourself. The only way to learn the former lesson is to start with the latter. Whether you identify with a goddess who represents transformation or a warrior sorceress, you can be sure she will show you how to embrace your own values and character. The resonance you feel within is key to working with any archetype, and this is no different for the Dark Goddess, either.

In some representations, the Dark Goddess archetype is the result of the unification of two opposing energies. The followers of these concepts rely on similar beliefs to Jung's model - the person is a whole made of two opposites within themselves. Likewise, practitioners of these traditions believe that by uniting the two divine powers, a new, more powerful divine energy is born. Unlike in other cultures, where the archetype is portrayed as something that undermines other forces (even benevolent divine ones), here, the goddess is emphatic and noble, capable of recognizing the need for balance in nature. This balance dictates that where there is light, there must be dark. Therefore, the opposing divine forces are both necessary and equal. While portrayed as fearsome and relentless, Dark Goddesses display an excellence of personal character - it's only a question of recognizing it. They are brave and courageous and ready to confront anyone they need to in the pursuit of winning the battle.

Those dabbling in alchemy and similar alternative practices believe that embracing the Dark Goddess archetype leads to a radical transformation, after which a person is better equipped to discover and cultivate empathy, love, and strength. While some of these qualities are not typically associated with dark female energies, the many representations of the archetype show that evoking Dark Goddesses often results in acquiring them and achieving personal and spiritual growth. By learning empathy when working with a Dark Goddess, one becomes more capable of understanding not only their own shortcomings but others' as well. After all, who better to teach you about acceptance than someone who is considered terrifying, deadly, and unapproachable? If you can accept them as they are, you can embrace your and other people's true personalities, whether they are sensed as terrible, awesome, relatable, unanimous, or in any other way.

In most cultures, the Dark Goddess archetype represents something inexplicable, intangible, and uncontrollable. This is another superb reason why working with them potentially benefits every spiritual seeker or even advanced practitioner. Often, what can be ascribed to these qualities is considered bad or evil - including parts of yourself. You have all these values within you, reminding you of your interconnectedness with everything in nature. Working with a Dark Goddess makes all of these seem more real and tangible. Many believe that archetypes can help deal with the unforeseen - many of the Dark Goddesses' actions were seen as such across the different myths and beliefs.

Those who previously feared the chaotic unknown that lies within them learned after working with a Dark Goddess (or the archetype itself) that just because there is something they didn't know about themselves, it doesn't mean they have to fear it. In contemporary portrayals, this archetype of dark feminine power became an indispensable tool for self-development. Besides dissuading your fears from the hidden parts of yourself, the Dark Goddesses can show you how to integrate them into your conscious psyche.

The Dark Goddess archetype symbolizes a more profound yet challenging side of people's existence, forces that shaped lives since the beginning of time. While interpretations and symbolism of these divine female energies vary across beliefs, these infinite variations are the reason people with individual needs can identify themselves with them. You can find your own way to work with one or more Dark Goddesses and embark on an eventful journey of discovery.

Chapter 2: Greek Goddesses

While the names of goddesses like Hera, who's known for being the queen of the gods, and Athena, the wise and strategic goddess of wisdom and warfare, roll off people's tongues effortlessly, there are some other intriguing, less well-recognized figures in Greek mythology. Persephone, Nyx, and Hekate are among them. These Dark Goddesses often bear the label of 'dark' or 'evil,' but understanding their origins and stories can shed light on their true natures.

Persephone, for example, is linked to the changing of seasons. Her tale begins with her being whisked away to the underworld by Hades, where she becomes his wife. This myth symbolizes the cycle of nature, where life goes through periods of dormancy and renewal. In the spring, Persephone returns to the Earth's surface, bringing with her the blossoms and beauty of the season. So, she's not really evil. She's more of a symbol of nature's perpetual cycle.

These Dark Goddesses often bear the label of "dark"', but understanding their stories can shed light on their true natures.

Nyx, the goddess of night, is a much older deity than the more famous Olympian gods and goddesses. She's the mother of several essential concepts, like Sleep and Death. Nyx isn't evil. She embodies the tranquility and rest that the night provides. Her dark embrace is a time for recharging and renewal.

Hekate, the goddess of crossroads, magic, and witchcraft, is another misunderstood figure. In ancient Greece, people invoked her at a crossroads to seek guidance and protection from evil spirits. Her association with magic sometimes led to her being portrayed as a sinister figure. However, she's a symbol of the knowledge and power found in the unknown and the choices you make in life.

These goddesses aren't truly evil or dark in the way you might think of villains. They represent different facets of life, like change, the mysteries of night, and the hidden wisdom within the world. They add layers of meaning to Greek mythology, and by exploring their stories, you can get a deeper appreciation for the complexities of life and nature. This chapter will help you explore the world of these dark Greek goddesses, especially from an esoteric perspective.

With so much literature available today, it's hard to separate the original stories from modified ones. However, learning how these goddesses were actually understood in their ancient context explains their significance and place. So, read on to unravel the hidden truths and untold tales of Persephone, Nyx, Hekate, and their mysterious counterparts, shedding light on the enigmatic and captivating aspects of Greek mythology that have long remained in the shadows.

Hecate/Hekate

Hekate, the goddess of crossroads, magic, and witchcraft.
Zde, CC BY-SA 4.0 <https://creativecommons.org/licenses/by-sa/4.0>, via Wikimedia Commons: https://commons.wikimedia.org/wiki/File:Relief_triplicate_Hekate_marble,_Hadrian_clasicism,_Prague_Kinsky,_NM-H10_4742,_151724.jpg

Hekate, the goddess of crossroads, magic, and witchcraft, has an ancient and mysterious history. She is one of the Titans, a group of primordial deities that predate the Olympian gods and goddesses. Her parents were Perses and Asteria, and she was often depicted as a triple goddess, representing the moon's three phases: the maiden, the mother, and the crone. This symbolism connects her to the cycles of life and the mysteries of the universe.

One of the most famous stories about Hekate centers on her role in the Titanomachy, the epic battle between the Titans and the Olympian gods. Hekate chose to remain neutral in this conflict, and, as a result, she was one of the few Titans to avoid imprisonment in the underworld after the Titans were defeated. Her neutrality and her ability to navigate the liminal spaces between light and dark, life and death, made her a unique and enigmatic figure.

Hekate's association with Crossroads is a central point of her mythology. In ancient Greece, travelers would often place offerings at crossroads to seek her protection and guidance. She was believed to have the power to open the gates between the mortal world and the spirit realm. This connection to crossroads symbolizes choices and transitions in life, emphasizing her role as a guide through life's uncertainties.

Hekate is also closely linked to magic and witchcraft. In the ancient world, she was often invoked during rituals and spells, particularly those associated with the moon and the night. Her torches illuminated the path in the darkness, both physically and metaphorically, guiding those who sought her wisdom and protection. She was considered a guardian of the mysteries of the occult, and her followers believed she could grant them knowledge and power. There are many myths surrounding this magical goddess, some of these include:

1. Hekate and the Abduction of Persephone

One of the most well-known myths involving Hekate is her role in the abduction of Persephone by Hades, which led to the changing seasons. According to the myth, Hades, the god of the underworld, fell in love with Persephone, the daughter of Demeter, the goddess of agriculture (more to be discussed later). When Hades abducted Persephone, Demeter was grief-stricken and wandered the Earth in search of her daughter. With her torches, Hekate helped Demeter in her search and played a crucial role in the reunion of mother and daughter. This myth highlights Hekate's connection to the underworld and her role as a guide in the realm of the dead.

2. The Role of Hekate in the Trojan War

Hekate also appears in the context of the Trojan War. She was believed to have aided the Greeks by providing them with guidance and protection during their long journey to Troy. The famous sorceress Medea, who was a priestess of Hekate, was said to have invoked the goddess's powers in her magical practices, demonstrating Hekate's role as a deity associated with magic and witchcraft.

3. Hekate's Encounter with Theseus

In another myth, the hero, Theseus, encountered Hekate when he was on his way to fight the Minotaur in the labyrinth. Hekate provided Theseus with guidance and protection during his perilous journey. She lit his path with her torches and offered him wisdom, ensuring his safe return from the labyrinth after defeating the Minotaur.

4. Hekate and the Dogs

Hekate is often illustrated accompanied by dogs, and in Greek mythology, it was believed that the sound of howling dogs was a sign of her presence. Dogs were considered sacred to her and often sacrificed in her rituals. Some myths even suggest that Hekate could transform into a dog, further emphasizing her close connection with these animals.

5. Hekate's Role in the Perseus and Medusa Myth

Hekate played a significant part in the tale of Perseus and Medusa. She assisted Perseus on his quest to slay the Gorgon Medusa. Hekate provided him with a polished shield to use as a mirror, enabling him to approach Medusa without directly looking at her and turning to stone. This myth underscores her association with powerful magical artifacts and her willingness to support heroes in their quests.

6. Hekate and the Protection of Newborns

Hekate was also revered as a protector of newborns and was often invoked during childbirth. It was believed that she could ward off evil spirits and ensure a safe delivery. Mothers would call upon Hekate to safeguard their infants during the vulnerable period of birth.

7. Hekate's Nightly Walks

Another intriguing belief about Hekate was that she was known to roam the Earth at night, particularly during the dark moon. During these nightly journeys, she was thought to be accompanied by a procession of restless spirits and the howling of dogs. People would leave offerings at crossroads to appease and seek her blessings during these nighttime excursions.

8. Hekate and the Golden Fleece

In the quest for the Golden Fleece, Hekate's assistance was sought by Jason and the Argonauts. It is said that she gave them knowledge and guidance to navigate the treacherous waters and challenges they encountered on their epic journey. This myth highlights her role as a source of wisdom and aid for heroes.

9. Hekate's Involvement in Orpheus' Quest

In the myth of Orpheus and Eurydice, when Orpheus descended into the underworld to rescue his beloved Eurydice, Hekate was one of the deities he encountered. Her presence in the underworld signified her influence over the realm of the dead and her role in guiding souls.

10. Hekate's Association with the Eumenides

Hekate was often linked with the Eumenides, also known as the Furies, who were vengeful spirits associated with the punishment of wrongdoers. Hekate acted as a mediator between the Eumenides and those who sought to appease them, reflecting her role as an intermediary between the human and divine realms.

Hekate, the goddess associated with the night, the dead, crossroads, and magic, is often viewed as a dark and enigmatic figure in Greek mythology. Her realm encompasses many elements that could be interpreted as mysterious and even foreboding, including her association with the occult, the spirit world, and the unseen forces of the cosmos. However, it is essential to recognize that Hekate was never inherently evil or malevolent, as her stories and deeds demonstrate.

Throughout Greek mythology and literature, Hekate consistently emerges as a guide, a protector, and a source of wisdom. She played pivotal roles in numerous heroic quests, aiding and offering insight to those who sought her assistance. Whether it was helping Perseus confront Medusa, guiding Jason in the quest for the Golden Fleece, or assisting

Aeneas in his journey to the underworld, Hekate showcased her benevolent side as a goddess who aided and protected those in need.

Hekate's connection to magic is often misunderstood. While she is associated with the mystical arts, it is crucial to remember that magic, like any tool, is not inherently good or evil; it depends on the intentions and actions of those who practice it. In her role as a guardian of magic, Hekate is neither good nor evil but is a source of knowledge and power for those who seek her guidance.

In essence, Hekate is a goddess of duality, representing the balance between light and dark, life and death, and the known and the unknown. Her mysteries and her multifaceted character reveal the complexities of existence, where she acts as a guiding force for those who find themselves at the crossroads of life.

Persephone

Persephone, the bringer of destruction.
Wolfgang Sauber, CC BY-SA 3.0 <https://creativecommons.org/licenses/by-sa/3.0>, via Wikimedia Commons: https://commons.wikimedia.org/wiki/File:AMI_-_Isis-Persephone.jpg

Persephone, the daughter of Demeter, the goddess of agriculture, and Zeus, the king of the gods, was a radiant and joyful young goddess. Her name, which means "bringer of destruction" or "bringer of death," foreshadows her eventual transformation into a dark deity. She was often described as a symbol of the bountiful Earth, radiating life and growth wherever she went.

Before her fateful encounter with Hades, Persephone enjoyed a carefree and idyllic life with her mother, Demeter. She spent her days in the meadows, nurturing the growth of flowers and crops, spreading beauty and abundance across the land. Her laughter and joy were said to have the power to make flowers bloom and fields flourish.

Persephone's abduction by Hades was a violent and sudden event. The earth literally cracked open, and Hades, in his dark chariot, emerged to seize her. Persephone's screams for help went unanswered as Hades took her to the depths of the underworld against her will. The stark element of her story is the contrast between her previous life in the bright, sunlit world and her abrupt descent into the shadowy realm of death.

Persephone's initial despair in the underworld is evident. She longed for her mother and the world above. However, as time passed, she assumed her role as the queen of the dead. She became a compassionate figure, bestowing solace to the souls in the afterlife. Her presence in the underworld signifies her strength and adaptability as she embraces her new role despite the initial hardship.

As Persephone was whisked away by Hades to the depths of the underworld, the world above mourned her absence. Her mother, Demeter, the goddess of agriculture, was grief-stricken. Consumed by despair, Demeter allowed the Earth to wither and the crops to die, and famine threatened the mortal realm.

1. Demeter's Quest to Find Her Daughter

Demeter, in her anguish, embarked on a relentless quest to find her beloved daughter. She searched high and low, appealing to the other gods for assistance. However, none could reveal Persephone's whereabouts, for it was a secret known only to the lord of the underworld.

2. Zeus' Intervention

Seeing the suffering of both the gods and mortals due to the barrenness of the Earth, Zeus, the king of the gods, intervened. He urged Hades to release Persephone, recognizing that her return to the surface world was essential to ending the famine.

3. The Compromise with the Pomegranate Seeds

Hades agreed to allow Persephone to return but presented a single condition. Since she had consumed six pomegranate seeds in the underworld, it was decreed that she must spend six months of each year with Hades. These months coincided with the winter season, during which the world would be shrouded in cold and darkness.

4. Persephone's Return and the Changing Seasons

Upon her return to the world above, Persephone's joyful reunion with her mother, Demeter, marked the beginning of spring. The Earth burst into life as flowers bloomed and crops flourished. The world reveled in the rebirth of nature and the return of Persephone.

5. The Waning of Life in the Underworld

During her absence from the underworld, the spirits of the dead longed for Persephone's return. The realm of the dead felt a waning of life and vitality as they missed the queen who offered them comfort and solace.

Persephone's story became a symbol of the eternal cycle of the seasons. Her time with Hades in the underworld marked the arrival of winter and the dormancy of the earth. Her reunions with Demeter aboveground signaled the renewal of life and the return of spring and summer.

Persephone's story reflects her dual nature. She is both the goddess of spring and growth when she is with her mother, Demeter, and the queen of the underworld during her time with Hades. This duality embodies the cycle of the seasons, with her descent into the underworld marking the arrival of winter and her return signifying the rebirth of spring.

Persephone as a Dark Goddess

Persephone's association with the underworld and her role as queen of the dead contribute to her reputation as a Dark Goddess. She is not evil, but her realm is one of shadows, death, and mystery. Her transformation from a carefree maiden into a powerful and enigmatic queen of the underworld underscores her dark aspect. Persephone's story also serves as a reminder of the delicate balance between life and death in the natural world.

Despite her dark associations, Persephone is not a malevolent deity. She is often depicted as a compassionate and fair ruler in the underworld, balancing the scales of justice and providing comfort to souls in the afterlife. Her annual return to the surface world heralds the rebirth of life and nature, symbolizing the cycle of renewal and growth.

Nyx

Nyx emerged from Chaos.
https://commons.wikimedia.org/wiki/File:BnF_MS_Gr139_folio_435_verso_-_detail_-_Nyx.jpg

Nyx, a goddess as old as time itself, emerged from Chaos, the primeval void from which the entire cosmos came forth. She was the embodiment of the night, the personification of darkness, and one of the original deities that predated even the mighty Olympian gods. She was a goddess of great depth, a figure of profound beauty veiled in an aura of darkness. Her dominion extended far beyond the physical night. She governed the abstract concepts associated with darkness, making her a deity of immense influence. In the realm of night, she presided over sleep, dreams, and even death.

One of the most fascinating aspects of Nyx was her many and diverse offspring. Among her notable children was Hypnos, the god of sleep, known for bringing rest and dreams to mortals. Another was Thanatos, the personification of death, representing the peaceful transition from life to the afterlife. Moros, the god of impending doom, underscored the inescapable fate that awaited all beings. Eris, the goddess of strife, thrived in the shadows, sowing discord and conflict often concealed under the cover of darkness. Apate, the deity of deceit, and Geras, representing the inevitable march of old age, were other offspring of Nyx. This diversity of her children emphasized the complexity of the forces Nyx presided over.

Nyx's presence in Greek mythology was all-pervasive, even though she did not feature as prominently as some other deities. She was often invoked during nighttime rituals when the world was shrouded in the mysteries of the dark. Nyx held immense power in her dominion over transitions, presiding over the shift from wakefulness to sleep, from life to death, and from consciousness to the ethereal world of dreams. Her influence was not only over the physical night but extended into the depths of the subconscious, the realm of dreams, and the enigmatic forces that governed existence. She was the true representation of a Dark Goddess.

In Greek mythology, there are some well-known and powerful goddesses like Athena and Aphrodite, but not much is said about the darker goddesses such as Nyx, Persephone, and Hekate. These figures are often associated with mystery and darkness, which might make people think they're evil. However, as you've explored their stories in this chapter, it's clear that they aren't necessarily evil. These Dark Goddesses are more complex than just being considered evil. Their stories reveal Greek mythology's depth and intricacy, showing that labels like "dark" or "evil" can be too simplistic to describe these multifaceted goddesses.

Chapter 3: Egyptian Goddesses

When one thinks of ancient Egyptian deities, only a few come to mind, like Cleopatra, Nefertiti, and Tutankhamun. However, there are many other gods and goddesses with fascinating powers and intriguing stories that you have probably never heard about before, like Sekhmet, Nephthys, Hathor, and Nut, the ancient Egyptian Dark Goddess.

Ancient Egyptian Dark Goddess.
https://pixabay.com/photos/hieroglyphs-goddess-queen-pharaoh-67471/

Sekhmet

Sekhmet means "one who is in control."

Sekhmet means "One who is in control" or "She who is powerful." It is a fitting name for one of the most powerful goddesses in ancient Egyptian mythology. She is referred to as the Mother Goddess and is part human, part animal. She is depicted as a woman with the face of a lion. There are many sculptures, amulets, and other monuments of Sekhmet which show her significance in ancient Egypt.

Sekhmet is a forgotten esoteric goddess. Esoteric deities have extraordinary abilities. So why is she a forgotten one? Sadly, not much is known about her, and she isn't mentioned in mythology as much as other deities. She remains an enigma. However, the few resources found about her praise her great but contradictory abilities. She could bring disease, chaos, and death while also administering healing and protection.

Mythology

Sekhmet was the daughter of the sun god Ra, the creator of the universe. In one legend, she was an incarnation of the sky goddess

Hathor. After Ra created mankind, he observed them from the skies. He had high hopes for his new creation, but he was disappointed to find they steered away from the right path and stopped following his rules of justice and order. He decided to punish them for their disobedience. He created Sekhmet from the fire in his eyes, which is why she is referred to as "The Eye of Ra." She was a weapon and a vengeful manifestation of his power that could breathe a fire hotter than the desert sun.

Ra sent Sekhmet to Earth to exact his punishment on mankind. She caused plagues across the lands. Using her fiery breath, Sekhmet set everything in her way on fire, killing almost all of mankind. Her bloodlust was out of control, and no one could stop her. Ra regretted his decision when he saw what his daughter did to his creation. He wasn't cruel or heartless. He only wanted to punish them and had no intention of killing them. If all mankind was destroyed, who would learn the lesson?

Ra commanded some of his priests to get red ochre and grind it with beer. They then poured it all over the land at night while Sekhmet was sleeping.

Sekhmet, who was bloodthirsty, mistook the red beer for blood and drank it all. She got intoxicated and fell asleep. When she woke up, she returned to Ra. In one legend, this was when he made her the goddess of war and chaos.

Attributes

Sekhmet is the goddess of war, chaos, healing, plague, and the hot desert sun. She is described in the Book of the Dead as a destructive and creative force. She has the power to bring plagues to mankind. As a healing goddess, she could be invoked to protect against diseases. There isn't a problem Sekhmet couldn't fix. She is the patron of healers and physicians. During wars, Sekhmet was the protector of the pharaohs and led them to victory.

Sekhmet has about 4,000 names that reflect her personality and attributes.

- Watcher and guardian of the West.
- Lady of the mountains.
- Lady of the Fire (because she breathes fire and protects the sun god, Ra).
- Lady of bright red linen (reflecting her bloodlust).

- Mistress of Ankh Tawy (another name for Memphis, the capital of ancient Egypt).
- Mistress of the tombs (reflecting her role as the Dark Goddess).
- Mistress of dread (for almost destroying mankind).
- The bloodthirsty.
- Lady of life (for her healing powers).
- Red lady (for sending plagues to mankind).

Roles

Sekhmet is responsible for bringing heat to the deserts, and she is called "Nesert," meaning flame. She brings suffering and disease but only to those who anger her. She guards Ra and also protects Ma'at, the goddess of balance and justice. Because of her fierce and terrifying nature, Sekhmet is called the "Lady of Terror."

Symbols

- Lioness
- Red linen
- Sun disk
- Cats

Sekhmet, the Dark Goddess

In ancient times, everyone feared Sekhmet, for she was the goddess of war. However, she is only threatening to those who disrespected her. She protected the ancient Egyptians by breathing fire and killing their enemies. However, when in battle, Sekhmet becomes blinded with rage and destroys everything in her way. Only drinking blood could calm her fiery anger.

Rituals/Worship

If you want to appease Sekhmet, burn incense, play music, or offer her food and drink.

Meditation Ritual

Instructions:

1. Build an altar for Sekhmet and place her pictures or symbols on its surface.
2. Light one or more candles.
3. Sit next to the altar in a comfortable position and close your eyes.

4. Take a few deep breaths and visualize Sekhmet.

5. Give yourself time until she either appears to you or you see any of her symbols.

6. Ask her for guidance.

Nephthys

Nephthys is one of the first Egyptian goddesses.
Jeff Dahl, CC BY-SA 4.0 <https://creativecommons.org/licenses/by-sa/4.0>, via Wikimedia Commons: https://commons.wikimedia.org/wiki/File:Nephthys.svg

Nephthys is one of the first Egyptian goddesses. She was born from the union between the Sky and the Earth after Ra created the universe. Nephthys is her Latin name, and her Egyptian name is *Nebthwt*, meaning "Mistress of the House" or "The Lady of the Temple."

Mythology

Osiris was the god of agriculture and fertility, and his wife, Isis, was the goddess of magic and light. They ruled over mankind together, and they were just and kind. Their sister, Nephthys, was married to their brother Set, the god of war. However, Nephthys had feelings for Osiris. One day, she transformed into Isis and seduced him, and they slept together. When Set found out, he thought that Osiris seduced and tricked Nephthys. Set already hated his brother and was very jealous of him, but after this incident, he planned to murder him. Set succeeded in his plan and killed his brother. He took his place as king with Nephthys by his side.

Isis was heartbroken over the loss of her husband and looked for his body everywhere. She wanted to bring him back to life so she could have his child. When she finally found him, she asked Nephthys to protect him from their evil brother, Set. However, Set figured out their plan and confronted Nephthys, who told him where they hid the body. Set took Osiris's body, cut it into little pieces, and threw them across the land.

When Isis returned, Nephthys felt guilty for betraying her trust. She promised to do everything in her power to fix her mistake. The sisters managed to find Osiris's parts and put him back together. They brought him back to life, and Isis got pregnant and had a son called Horus.

She kept him hidden away from Set. Nephthys, who learned from her mistake, didn't reveal her sister's secret to anyone. She nursed Horus and helped Isis raise him. When Horus grew up and took back his throne, he made Nephthys the head of his family and his chief counselor. Because of this myth, many Egyptians consider Nephthys a nursing mother and a symbol of guidance and protection.

Attributes

Nephthys is depicted as a woman with the symbol of her name over her head. Her illustrations were present in many ancient tombs because she protected the dead and attended Osiris's mummification.

Roles

She is associated with darkness, twilight, and the setting sun. She is the goddess of the air, sky, heaven, and hell. She protects the dead from evil spirits by transforming into a kite and wails to mourn the departed. She guarded the coffins and the canopic jars where the deceased organs were stored. She originally protected Hapi, god of the Nile, jars but later became protector of all containers.

Symbols

- Sycamore trees
- Temples

- Hawks
- Glacons
- Woman with wings.
- Kites
- Beer

Nephthys, the Dark Goddess

Nephthys is the goddess of death and is associated with decay. She helps the souls of the departed cross over to the other side. She takes care of these spirits even after she escorts them to the afterlife. She comforts their families during their mourning period and lets them know that their loved ones are safe and in a good place. This is why she is called "Friend of the Dead." In fact, she is the only goddess to care about the dead and treat them with love and kindness.

Her followers often call on her after the death of a loved one, so she is present during funerals to guard the dead. Nephthys has magical abilities that resemble Isis, the goddess of magic and healing. Isis is a force of light, and Nephthys is a force of darkness, so they balance each other.

Nephthys also became the goddess of birth after giving birth to Anubis, the god of death.

Rituals/Worship

Invoke Nephthys with his visualization technique.

1. Find a quiet room and sit in a comfortable position.
2. Close your eyes and put your hands together, then place them on your heart.
3. Take a long, deep breath and visualize the light of Nephthys flowing through every part of your body.
4. Breathe out and feel her light beneath your feet.
5. Take a long, deep breath and feel her light filling your heart.
6. Vibrate her name, then slowly open your hands and let her light fill your space.
7. If you feel her presence, ask her any question you have.
8. After you have finished, express your gratitude to her.

Hathor

Hathor's name means "Temple of Horus."
Jeff Dahl, CC BY-SA 4.0 <https://creativecommons.org/licenses/by-sa/4.0>, via Wikimedia Commons: https://commons.wikimedia.org/wiki/File:Hathor.svg

Hathor is associated with Sekhmet, and some historians believe that Sekhmet is derived from her. She is depicted either as a cow or a woman with a cow's head. Hathor is Ra's daughter and was highly venerated among the ancient Egyptians. Her name means "Temple of Horus," which refers to how Horus (the sun god) enters her mouth every night to sleep and then wakes up the next morning to light the sky. This myth explains how the sun shines and sets every day.

Mythology

Hathor was an image of love and kindness. However, before that, she used to have a much darker side. In some legends, Ra sent Hathor to punish mankind for their disobedience. After she unleashed her vengeance and destroyed everything and everyone, as a result of her evil doings, she transformed into Sekhmet. When she woke up from this intoxication, she was back to being Hathor. However, she had changed and became a better, kinder, and calmer version of herself.

The goddess who wanted to annihilate the world became an ally to mankind. She blessed them with many gifts and helped the less fortunate. Whenever they prayed to her, she would come through for them. She became the mother goddess, and all the other goddesses are believed to be her avatars.

In another myth, when Horus grew up, he wanted to claim the throne from his uncle Set. Since Set was cunning and untrustworthy, Horus took his case to the counsel of gods who were led by Ra. However, Ra couldn't see eye to eye with one of the gods. So, he became angry and refused to participate in the trial.

Hathor knew that her father's anger could bring the end of the world. So she visited him, and in an unexpected move, she revealed her genitals. He was amused and aroused, and his anger subsided. He then went back to court to handle Horus's case.

This story highlights the significance of masculinity and femininity. When both are in harmony, they bring balance to the universe.

Attributes

Hathor is the goddess of love, celebration, music, dance, motherhood, gratitude, drunkenness, and joy, similar to Venus and Aphrodite from Roman and Greek mythology. She is also the patron of women and their health.

She is also the ruler of childbirth, the East, the West, fertility, agriculture, the moon, the sun, and the sky.

Roles

Hathor has many different roles. She is responsible for renewing the cosmos, helping women give birth, and resurrecting the dead. She is also a lunar deity and guides the boats at night till they reach the shore safely. In ancient Egypt, night was a metaphor for death. So, it is also believed that she illuminates the way for the deceased to reach their final resting place.

Symbols

- Cow
- Cow's ears

- Cow horns
- Solar disk
- Papyrus plant
- Sycamore tree
- Serpent
- Lioness

Hathor the Dark Goddess

Hathor holds the great honor of being the goddess of the afterlife in The Field of Reeds. It is a place similar to the concept of paradise where the dead spend their eternity with their loved ones without any pain or suffering.

When a good woman or girl dies, she assumes the likeness of Hathor before crossing to the Field of Reeds.

Rituals/Worship

Connect with Hathor by making any of these offerings:

- Roses
- Cedar
- Cinnamon
- Myrrh
- Wine
- Beer
- Butter
- Cheese
- Bread
- Dates
- Figs
- Freshwater
- Jasmine, chamomile, or rose oil.
- Perfumes
- Gold
- Copper

You can also set an altar in her honor. Keep the decoration simple; a picture or statue of her and a red or white candle will be enough.

Nut

Nut, the goddess of the sky.

Nut is the daughter of Shu, the god of air, and Tenfut, the goddess of rainfall and moisture. She is Ra's granddaughter and married to Geb, the god of the earth. Nut is the goddess of the sky and one of the most significant deities in ancient mythology.

The name "Nut" means water, and she is depicted with a water pot on her head.

Mythology

When Ra created Nut (the sky) and Geb (the earth), they were close and had non-stop sex. They were unable to let each other go. Although their love was so strong, this closeness prevented Nut from having children. Geb and Nut's father, Shu, wanted her to give birth to his grandchildren. He was also jealous of Geb and Nut's close relationship, so he forced them to separate. This was how the separation of the sky and Earth was explained in ancient Egyptian mythology.

In another myth, Ra loved Nut and wanted to marry her. However, she was in love with Geb and they were sleeping together. When Ra found out, he cursed her so she could never have children in any month of the year.

Nut went to Thoth, the god of wisdom, and sought his help. He was fond of her, so he devised a plan to help her break the curse. He challenged Koshnu, the goddess of the moon, to a game of checkers. They kept making bets and placing wagers on each match. Thoth won the game, and Koahnu gave him a part of her illumination. Thoth used it to add five extra days to the year. Since they didn't belong to any month, Nut was able to cheat Ra's curse. She gave birth to Osiris, Isis, Seth, and Nephthys.

Nut also helped Ra ascend to the sky. Ra decided to abdicate his throne and retire to the skies. However, he was so old and weak and couldn't make the journey on his own. Nun asked Nut to carry Ra on her back and bring him to the skies. However, Ra was very large, and Nut didn't believe she could carry him by herself. So Nun transformed her into a cow that Ra rode and reached the skies.

Attributes

Nut is depicted as a beautiful naked woman with wings standing in the skies and is covered in drawings of stars.

Roles

Nut protects the world from Nun, the water of creation. She also gave birth to four members of the Great Enneads. They were the first nine gods in ancient Egyptian mythology: Ra, Shu, Tefnut, Geb, Nut, Osiris, Isis, Seth, and Nephthys.

She used to be the goddess of the night sky and was associated with the Milky Way. Over time, her role changed, and she became the goddess of all skies.

Symbols

- Sky
- Cow
- Stars

- Freedom
- Omnipotence
- Wisdom
- Abundance
- Eternity
- Immortality
- Frogs
- Bunnies
- Bees
- Lotus flowers
- Opal
- Blue Topaz
- Tourmaline
- Sapphire
- Blue
- Black

The Dark Goddess Aspect

Nut is the goddess of sarcophagi and coffins. She watches over the dead until their rebirth in the afterlife.

Rituals/Worship

Practice this ritual if you want to invoke Nut.

1. Choose a place outdoors under the night sky, or you can set up an indoor altar with night symbols like stars, constellations, or the moon.
2. Light a white or blue candle.
3. Place any of Nut's symbols on the altar.
4. Make an offering to Nut.
5. Meditate next to the altar by closing your eyes and focusing on your breathing.
6. Clear your mind and visualize Nut.
7. Ask her for guidance and be ready to receive her wisdom.

Nut and Kemetic Spirituality

Kemetic spirituality is a belief inspired by ancient Egyptian religion that focuses on the connection between mankind and the divine and the belief that the universe is an extension of yourself.

The ancient religion is based on the circle of life that Nut represents. Every night, she swallows the sun god and then gives birth to him the next morning. She also swallows the moon every morning and gives birth to her at night.

The dark ancient Egyptian goddesses embody a number of characteristics. They can be bloodthirsty and a force of destruction and also guides and protectors. They represent a complex, multi-faced nature of ancient Egyptian mythology, where light and darkness and creation and destruction are intertwined in a complex cosmic tapestry.

Chapter 4: Mesopotamian Goddesses

In this chapter, you'll find an in-depth exploration of the Mesopotamian Dark Goddesses, Ereshkigal, Lilith, and Inanna. Besides examining the different aspects of the divine feminine, as expressed through their mythology, roles, and qualities, you'll also learn about their symbol as a Dark Goddess.

Lilith

Lilith appears in numerous cultures and traditions.
Manuel Parada López de Corselas User:Manuel de Corselas ARS SUMMUM, Centro para el Estudio y Difusión Libres de la Historia del Arte, Public domain, via Wikimedia Commons :
https://commons.wikimedia.org/wiki/File:Lilith_Periodo_de_Isin_Larsa_y_Babilonia.JPG

Also known as Lillake, Lilitu, Belili, and Baalat, Lilith appears in numerous cultures and traditions. Her most prominent role is tied to Jewish mythology, which claims she was Adam's first wife. According to the tale, Lilith refused to submit to her husband's wishes because she believed they should be equal. As a result, she left Adam but was cursed to bear only demons instead of children. Some claim that she later returned to the paradise she abandoned, turned herself into a snake and caused Adam and his new wife, Eve, to be expelled too. However, the origins of this myth can be traced back to the Sumero-Babylonian Goddess who had the same dark and frivolous qualities as she is given in the rabbinical tales. Here, too, Lilith is described as a screeching demon, either accompanied by an owl or turning into one, lurking during the night and attacking unsuspecting men and children. Since she can't have her own children, she takes her fury out on others by killing them. The Canaanites, on the other hand, held her in high regard, addressing her as the "Divine Lady." Perhaps it was the combination of all these myths that led to the emergence of Lilith as the goddess of rebellion, independence, and innate sexuality.

One of her earliest mentions is on a clay tablet from Ur, dating back to 2000 B.C., but based on mythology, her roots can be traced back to Sumer, 3000 B.C. Later folklore puts her origins at a much earlier date, in 700 B.C., when she was first called Lilith, the name under which she is known today. In some Babylonian legends, Lilith is known as the Maid of Desolation or Dark Maid. She either works with the creatures of the night, terrorizing people or is one of them (as a vampire or demon). Despite her demonlike features, claws, and bird feet, she is so beautiful and enchanting that no man who encounters her can resist her. In rituals, Lilith can be represented by red jasper, garnet, carnelian, or any other orange or red crystals that convey passion and sensuality.

According to a Sumerian Legend, Lilith was jealous of Inanna, the goddess of war and love. When Inanna planted a sacred tree she wanted to make her throne, Lilith flew onto the tree in a bird form, preventing Inanna from taking residence. Some claim Lilith's actions were deliberate attempts to obstruct Inanna from reaching her full power (Innana was afraid of birds, and Lilith knew she wouldn't dare to go on a tree occupied by a bird). However, the hero Gilgamesh comes to Inanna's rescue, driving Lilith out and enabling Innana to take her rightful place.

Due to her sexual symbolism, in Ancient Mesopotamian culture, Lilith is also associated with breasts. Being a powerful female demon, Lilith is said to cause diseases affecting women, preventing them from breastfeeding their children and causing them to die. This is likely related to her inability to bear and nurse children, which may have driven her to want to prevent other women from doing the same.

As an archetype of an empowering Dark Goddess, Lilith is seen as the goddess of Wild Freedom. She teaches her followers that they must be willing to embrace who they truly are and trust that those who are meant to accept them will come in time. While she acknowledged that this is sometimes easier said than done, she encourages everyone to maintain self-sovereignty even when they're shamed and cast aside for their thoughts, feelings, or actions. No outside validation is worth sacrificing who you are within or abandoning the love you have for yourself.

Moreover, Lilith teaches her followers that instead of submitting to others' will and needs, they become the ones who hold and uplift those who are pushed aside by society. She encourages them to devote themselves to a fierce passion that supports their tender quality instead of suffocating it. In a sense, Lilith is one of the most rewarding Dark Goddesses to work with as she helps worshippers become closer to the divine feminine archetype they identify with.

At the same time, Lilith doesn't discourage anyone from completely disregarding their loved ones' needs. She fosters raising one's standard instead and finding a way to appreciate these demands while taking care of one's own needs. She teaches how to make the seed of a woman's inner wisdom and values blossom, finding balance in this world full of diversity. Lilith acknowledges that ambivalent feelings toward meeting one's needs are born from an inner dark void.

This dark aspect of Lilith seems dangerous and intense, but it doesn't have to be. While it's true that following this dark feminine power can generate many negative experiences, it's necessary in order to find a balance in life. Lilith can drive you to seek conflicts without a valid reason (other than seeking attention), become irritated with everyone who expresses different points of view, become domineering, selfish, and boastful, and disregard other people's needs. In modern terms, she is like a psychic vampire (an apt name given her portrayal in mythology), draining people of energy and the will to live. You need to exercise extreme caution to prevent yourself from falling into the trap of disregarding her positive lessons and using her power for selfish reasons.

Whether seen as a mixture of light and dark or a completely dark one, in all cultures she appeared, Lilith seems to provide a form of liberation to those she encountered. For example, by seducing men, as described in Mesopotamian mythology, she gave them a sense of uninhibited freedom from moral constraints. While some may argue that her methods were exceedingly radical, they have been shown to be necessary to make people face the consequences they were unprepared or unwilling to handle.

Inanna

Inanna is known by Sumerians as "the lady of the heavens."
Sailko, CC BY 3.0 <https://creativecommons.org/licenses/by/3.0>, via Wikimedia Commons: https://commons.wikimedia.org/wiki/File:Ishtar_on_an_Akkadian_seal.jpg

Known by the Sumerians as "the lady of the heavens," Inanna is one of the most complex and mysterious of all dark deities. She is thought to be the daughter of Ningal and Anu and the twin sister of Ereshkigal, another Dark Goddess from Mesopotamian mythology. In some myths, Inanna is pushed into an arranged marriage to Dumuzi, while in others, she is unmarried, and Dumuzi is only her consort. Either way, she was keen to maintain her boundaries with him, which went against her temptress aura in the Epic of Gilgamesh, where she wanted to take the hero who saved her as a lover but was rejected by him.

Inanna's traits are just as contradictory as the tales about her actions and roles. Known by many as an influential, ambitious, and empowering goddess, she also seems to be a shy maiden whose potential and freedom are restricted by the patriarchal society she lives in. There is, however, a focal point in all of her stories, and this is her sexuality. Her sensual nature is evident in various pieces of Mesopotamian poetry and tales, with people praying to her when they needed help with impotence or unrequited love. Some even went as far as claiming her to be the patron of the ladies of the night.

Inanna is also associated with art and is often illustrated in art pieces nude or wearing a cape and slightly revealing her nude figure underneath. By contrast, in other depictions, she is wearing a trimmed robe and has weapons peeking out from under her shoulders, indicating her passion for warfare. She may also hold a weapon in her hands and even be illustrated with a beard to emphasize her masculinity, as it was believed that to be a successful leader in a battle, you had to be male.

Inanna's preference for military functions wasn't evident before the Old Akkadian period when scripts mainly focused on her femininity. Some theorize that the masculine and war-like aspects were used as additional leverage for exercising political power when her feminine nature wasn't enough to sway people over.

Innana is often represented by a bundle of reeds standing in front of two gate posts. She can also be seen standing on a lion's back. She is associated with the colors red and blue and the stones carnelian and lapis lazuli. Some claim that red and blue signify her feminine and masculine natures, respectively. An eight-pointed star is sometimes used to symbolize the goddess's transcendent nature.

According to a myth, Inanna was attacked by a gardener while she was sleeping under a tree. Infuriated, she embarked on a long journey to find the gardener who went into hiding. Her journey is often likened to that of Venus' astral path.

In another story, Inanna journeys to the underworld and back. There, she sits on Ereshkigal's throne, which angers the other deities in the pantheon, who then kill her for her insolence. After her helper, Ninšubur, asked for Enki's help, the two of them brought Inanna back to the world. Due to her trips back and forth from the world of the dead, Inanna became associated with the journey to the afterlife in Assyrian mythology.

However, because it is never that simple in mythology, other tales claim that Inanna only wanted to patch things up with her estranged sister and paid a high price for it. At the time it occurred to her to visit Ereshkigal in the underworld, Inanna was already a celebrated ruler and a celebrated goddess. She was blessed with beauty, power, and influence and seemingly had it all. Yet, after being at odds with her twin for so long, she was compelled to leave their differences behind. She felt she was denying parts of herself and needed to reclaim them. As she was traveling to the underworld, Inanna was stopped at each of the seven gates of the underworld. At each stop, she was stripped more and more of her possessions, powers, and parts of her identity. When finally reunited with her sister, Inanna wasn't a welcomed guest. Having just lost her husband, Ereshkigal wasn't in the mood to patch things up with her sister (although some tales claim that Ereshkigal's husband's death was caused by Inanna's actions). Wanting Inanna to leave her alone, Ereshkigal left her sister to die by hanging her up on a deadly hook. However, Inanna's guides traveled to the underworld and, after comforting Ereshkigal as she was mourning her husband, they convinced her to give Inanna's body back to them so they could take her back to the world of the living.

According to yet another version of the story, Inanna was revived by the red waters of life, emerging from the underworld with even more power and influence. It's unclear whether this power had been bestowed upon her deliberately by her twin or was a result of her revival from the dead. This version of Inanna's journey to the underworld relates most closely to her Dark Goddess archetype. As the dark feminine, she teaches her followers that there is a hidden desire to explore the repressed parts of the self in everyone. Sometimes, people don't understand what compels others to seek out the darkest parts of themselves or act in a way that results in the same.

As a Dark Goddess, Inanna encourages one to take one's own "Underworld Journey," exploring the deepest, most hidden parts that the ego doesn't want to acknowledge. Instead of layers of projection, understanding, and satisfaction with blanket truths about one's darkest traits, she fosters seeking them out, even if they lead to pain caused by the death of the ego. Just as Inanna was stripped of everything that kept her ego alive, so will everyone who confronts their shadow self. However, as these hidden pockets are often filled with repressed grief, exploring them can lay a foundation for healing in a healthy way.

It takes a truly courageous person to surrender more fully to the darkness without knowing what they will encounter. However, by illuminating these dark spaces, you can unravel negative emotions caused by past trauma, like shame, guilt, denial, and delusion of separation, and eventually unearth the empowering compassion. By embracing the darkest side she was compelled to explore, Inanna was able to reclaim her title among the living and emerge as an even more powerful queen and goddess than she was before. And just as she was able to gain empowerment by reclaiming everything within her, so can everyone who chooses to work with her as a Dark Goddess.

Ereshkigal

Ereshkigal is the goddess of the underworld in Mesopotamian mythology. Being the ruler of the land of the dead, Ereshkigal is associated with death, transformation, and the mysteries of the afterlife. "Ereshkigal" translates to "Queen of the Great Place/Below." According to legend, while the souls who ended up in her realm ate dust and drank mud, Ereshkigal resided in a palace built of lapis lazuli, enticing the dead souls to come to her. Once they were in her realm, Ereshkigal kept the souls there and refused to release them. Some claimed that she prevented mortals from learning about the underworld and the afterlife and prevented them from entering her realm. Her palace, Ganzir, has seven gates and is located near the gates of the land of the dead. Ereshkigal was the sole queen of the underworld until she took the deity Nergal, who became her confidant and consort and helped her rule the underworld.

As feared as she was for her role as the keeper of the dead and the queen of the underworld, Ereshkigal was also highly esteemed and respected by her followers. She's featured in the myth of the Descent of Inanna, which concludes by celebrating Ereshkigal.

Like her sister, Ereshkigal was also associated with dark sensuality, as witnessed by her portrayal as a winged naked woman in ancient terra-cotta plates. The woman carries symbols of all-encompassing power with her wings pointing downward. Standing with two owls on either side, her feet are shaped like talons, and she stands on two lions that lie on top of the mountains. According to other illustrations, Ereshkigal reigned over the vast wilderness of the underworld, which is why she was associated with wild creatures. Besides lions and owls, she is also portrayed holding feathers, snakes, and gemstones like lapis lazuli. However, her illustrations are rare as Mesopotamians only created depictions of something they wanted to bring attention to, which wasn't the case with a goddess they feared.

Being the Queen of the Underworld, it's easy to see why Ereshkigal fits the archetype of the Dark Goddess. She is the perfect embodiment of the journey through and toward the shadow. While she beckoned the departed souls toward her, she could also summon the courage, power, and light one needs to let go of grief and hurt. Those who hear her call or are curious to work with her also claim that Ereshkigal is an excellent source of empowerment during ancestral healing or worship practices.

Ereshkigal encourages everyone to have an open mind and heart, even toward the pain that looking back to the past inevitably brings. She reminds everyone that while meeting their deepest pain is challenging, it doesn't mean they have to look for solutions to dispel this feeling right away. In fact, in these cases, quick fixes don't do any good but can delay the healing process. What they truly need is compassion, love, understanding, and being present in the emotion to process it. Ereshkigal also asserts that when they accept that embracing pain is part of the rebirth process, they reemerge with more clarity. Some claim that when Ereshkigal fully embraced her pain, she experienced this revival, which brought her sister back to life. At the same time, it allowed her to heal after her husband's death as well.

Ereshkigal teaches her followers to nurture the pain in their shadow so they can turn it into a power and ability to share their gifts with the world. Any demon (ill thoughts, emotions, or behaviors) a person projects outwardly is a mirror of the pain they have yet to embrace within.

Holding the key to liberation, Ereshkigal demands that you face all trepidations, one by one, as a means to learn to cope with the uncertainty, despair, and grief that can accompany them. Once this happens, the person is free of pain and everything else they've kept hidden, which blocks them from living life fully.

They've embraced the darkness within themselves and their ability to explore the shadows and face the darkness hidden in them. As a Dark Goddess, Ereshkigal teaches that the fear of what others say when you decide to embrace your shadow and pain holds a much tighter hold on you than the pain itself. The more a person lets in the pain, the easier it becomes to accept that it won't kill them. Even if it seems that you die a thousand deaths while working through the pain, you will be revived and reemerge pain-free in the end.

This Dark Goddess's lessons for embracing pain highlight the importance of reclaiming sovereignty from within. Ereshkigal prompts those willing to learn from her to reclaim their inner darkness with the same reverence with which they would see their positive aspects. By providing the power for self-empowerment, she helps strengthen your relationship with others and with yourself.

Chapter 5: Slavic Goddesses

Ancient Slavic lore poses a lot of challenges for historians who wish to explore it, as there are no original written records of their deities, rituals, celebrations, tales, or prayers. Most of the knowledge they possess today comes from secondary sources recorded by monks during the Christianization of the region.

The origins of Slavic mythology can be found in Proto-Indo-European times. According to some researchers, these stories could even date back to the Neolithic period. The Slavs of old were split up into local tribes, each with its own mythology, gods, and beliefs. Even the stories and customs of those who lived in the East were similar to those of the Iranians at the time.

Indigenous oral storytelling and religious practices were replaced by Christianity in the late 12th century when Bishop Absalon and his Danish troops invaded the region. His destruction of the statue of Svantevit, the god of war and abundance, marked the end of ancient Slavic paganism.

There are numerous remarkable deities in the Slavic pantheon. However, this chapter will focus on two of the most famous yet highly misunderstood dark female figures in Slavic mythology, Baba Yaga and Marzanna, along with their aspects. Reading this chapter, you will understand the etymology of their names, learn about their characteristics and the accompanying symbolism, explore the roles they play in folklore, and find out about the rituals and celebrations associated with them.

Slavic Goddess.

Baba Yaga

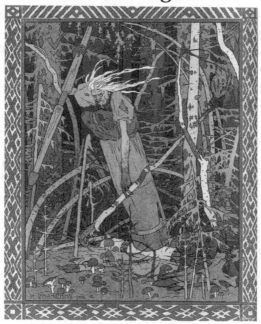

Baba Yaga is a notorious witch in Slavic folklore.

Originating in Slavic folklore, Baba Yaga is a notorious witch and the ancient deity of old bones who inhabited a mystical den in the vast forest. While she was feared for eating and imprisoning people, especially children, the mythological creature also served as a symbol of female empowerment. According to folklore, the witch also guarded the water of life, which is a powerful liquid that can resurrect the dead.

While Baba Yaga or Jaga is generally understood as the "Grandmother Witch," there is a lot of uncertainty surrounding the true etymology and meaning of the term. "Baba" is a babble word that translates to "old woman." The same word is still used in Bulgaria, Serbia, Croatia, and other nearby countries in the region to refer to "grandmother." Derivatives of the term, which carry mostly negative connotations, are also used in Ukraine and Poland today.

Etymology

The term "Yaga," however, still raises many questions as it points to no clear etymology. That said, other Slavic languages possess similar sounding vocabulary, such as the terms "jeza," which means "horror" or "anger" in Croatian and Slovenian, and "jedza," which means "witch" in Polish. The oldest mention of Baba Yaga was in 1755 in Mikhail V. Lomonosov's book on Russian Grammar. However, it is generally believed that she existed in the tradition of oral Slavic folklore storytelling long before that. In the book, the grandmother witch was mentioned alongside other Slavic deities. Even though the Slavic gods were mentioned with their equivalents from the Roman pantheon, Baba Yaga appeared without an equivalent.

Characteristics and Symbolism

Baba Yaga is shown with iron teeth with sharp edges, a very long nose, and long and thin legs of clay. The witch has a thin, bony body and engages in activities that are not conventionally woman-like. This strips away all elements of femininity from her. Instead of flying around on a broom, the witch transports herself in a mortar, rows it with a pestle, and uses the broom to sweep her tracks away.

The mortar and pestle are much more than modes of transportation but are believed to carry strong symbolism. Using these instruments to grind flax, which was then used to spin cloth, was a popular craft among women and was an ironic means of transportation for Baba Yaga, considering that it carried heavy feminine connotations. The mortar and pestle also traditionally symbolize birth, creation, nurture, and death.

Baba Yaga is a very complex and intriguing character. Although she shows up in many tales and plays pivotal roles in them, the old witch's true intentions, motivations, and desires remain unknown. She is helpful yet chaotic and often very vicious, leaving protagonists wishing they hadn't reached out for her help even if they got what they wanted. She is also believed to eat whoever fails to complete her tests and tasks. People can sense Baba Yaga's presence before she appears as she is accompanied by wild winds that cause trees to creak.

Baba Yaga lives in a hut deep in the mystical forest, like most other witches. However, the grandmother witch's hut stands out because it stands on its own pair of enormous chicken legs, allowing it to roam around the forest and search for those who need Baba Yaga's help. The house groans and screams with every move, signifying its terrible state and ominous feel. According to folklore, the hut is a living entity with its own personality.

The hut is surrounded by human bones and skulls. There are human legs and hands for wooden poles and a mouth with sharp teeth for a keyhole. Dangerous, carnivorous dogs guard the hut from intruders. What many people don't know is that Baba Yaga has two sisters, who are also Baba Yagas. In a sense, the Baba Yagas become the archetype of the triple goddess together. The grandmother witch symbolizes death and represents the aspect of the crone in the triple goddess deity archetype, while her sisters represent the aspects of the virgin and the mother.

Baba Yaga possesses unparalleled power as the guardian of the Water of Life and Death. If someone is killed in battle, for instance, Baba Yaga can use the Water of Death to heal all the wounds before using the Water of Life to bring them back to life. In many of the stories in which Baba Yaga appears, a magical oven plays a significant role. The oven has been seen as a symbol of the womb, representing life and birth, since the beginning of time. The oven is also associated with bread, symbolizing the Earth. The Earth is where the body is buried, which is often the step before rebirth or reincarnation, depending on each person's spiritual beliefs.

Despite her viciousness, the witch never goes after people unless they seek her out or provoke her. Most villains in tales and folklore are inherently evil and either feed off cruelty or have lofty motives such as world dominion, while the protagonists are entirely good and have heroic intentions.

On the other hand, Baba Yaga is presented in a neutral light, which is a lot more realistic. The witch doesn't have a moral compass guiding her through life, and her motives are unclear, which is why she doesn't feel the need to engage in either good or evil activities. When someone reaches out to her, she is willing to help them once they prove themselves worthy of her help. If they don't, then she'll do horrible things to them because she has no sense of morality.

Folklore Features

Baba Yaga often serves as the villain in any tale she's featured in. However, the more you delve into folklore, the more you'll appreciate how she's conveyed as a trickster who evokes change and transformation rather than being a stereotypically evil old crone. Her most famous appearances are in the story *Vasilissa the Beautiful,* where Vasilissa's stepmother sends her to Baba Yaga in search of her fire. On visiting the witch, Vasilissa undergoes a series of tests and quests that she manages to complete. Baba Yaga grants her the fire. However, when Vasilissa returns home, the fire ends up burning and killing her family as a consequence of their cruelty.

She also appears in *The Frog Princess and Baba Yaga,* where a prince marries a frog who he finds out is actually a beautiful woman. However, she ends up leaving him when he betrays her trust. He then goes on a mission to prove himself worthy to her so he can earn her forgiveness. The prince encounters Baba Yaga several times on his quest, who instigates transformations and helps progress the plot.

Marzanna

Marzanna, the Goddess of Winter and Death.

Marzanna, the Goddess of Winter and Death and the patroness of the underworld, goes by many names like Morana, Marzena, and Morena. Ceres, the Roman goddess of agriculture and fertility, and Hecate, the Greek goddess of witchcraft, necromancy, and night, are Marzanna's equivalents. She is related to Zhiva, the goddess of summer, and Lada, the Spring goddess. She is also Triglav's, the god of war, mother.

One of the most popular folktales regarding the cycle of the seasons is the marriage of Marzanna and Jarylo, the god of spring, war, and agriculture. According to this tale, Marzanna, the daughter of Mokosz, the great mother, and Perun, the god of thunder, was once the goddess of nature. When she was young, Jarylo, who turns out to be her brother, was kidnapped by another deity and taken to the underworld. On his return, neither Marzanna nor Jarylo knew that they were twins. The siblings ended up falling in love and getting married.

Nothing restored balance in the world like their marriage did. Alas, they were the deities of nature and agriculture. However, this peace was short-lived. Marzanna killed Jarylo when he cheated on her, which turned her into the cold, fearful deity of death and nature. Jarylo's death during the fall and the end of their marriage were what initiated the arrival of winter.

Dziewanna, the goddess of spring, and Jarylo then returned to kill Marzanna during the spring, triggering the onset of summer. According to lore, this cycle happens every year, creating the cycle of changing seasons. Neither Jarylo, who symbolizes summer, nor Mazanna, who represents winter, can exist or survive at the same time.

Etymology

The name Marzanna is derived from the Proto-Indo-European term "mar," which means death. Many researchers and folklorists believe that the deity is associated with Mars, the Roman deity of war, as his name also evolved from the Latin term "mors," which also translates to death. His name could also be tied to the Russian word "more," which means "pestilence." Marzanna is linked to Mars because the war deity was originally the god of agriculture in the Roman pantheon.

Other folklorists suggest that Marzanna is related to "Mare," an evil spirit found in Slavic and Germanic mythology. Like Marzanna, Mare, too, was thought to create nightmares and accompany sleep paralysis. The Ukrainian term "mara" translates to "dream" and means "hallucinations" in some Slavic languages.

Characteristics and Symbolism

Researchers suggest that Marzanna is a remnant of broader deity archetypes from regional pantheons, such as the monstrous deity Merihem and Marah, the Canaanite goddess of war. In Slavic mythology, Marzanna is deeply feared as she is believed to attract death. Her appearance also symbolizes the beginning of the winter season. The deity represents the harsh and frigid nature of the season. Her association with both death and the onset of winter symbolizes the end of the natural cycle of humans, the seasons, and agricultural practices.

Winter is also generally representative of dormancy and death, as plants wither, trees lose their leaves, and the overall environment, once vibrant, appears lifeless. In many societies, especially those that rely on agriculture, winter is the most dreaded time of year. People eagerly await spring when the growing season returns.

Before Christianity grew popular in the Slavic region, people were commonly found praying and worshiping Marzanna to bless them with an abundant harvest. There were several rituals and ceremonies dedicated to the deity. They also used symbols like ice, snow, and wooden dolls or ones made of straw and similar natural materials to represent the goddess. Marzanna was thought to die at the end of the winter, also signaling the rebirth of the spring goddess, Lada, and the arrival of spring.

Marzanna sometimes appears in one of her different guises, as Mora, who is the personification of fate. This face of the deity is a malevolent hag who is often regarded as an incarnation of the evil spirit. She leaves her victims breathless and feeds off the blood of men. She is described as a shapeshifting tormentor. She can turn herself into anything, from a large, majestic horse to an unassuming lock of hair.

One tale tells the story of a man who was so repulsed by Marzanna that he ended up fleeing his home. He stormed off on his horse, but little did he know that the deity followed him everywhere he went because she disguised herself as his horse. He eventually grew weary and decided to rest at an inn. When he heard the man groaning at night, the host decided to go into his bedroom. He thought the man was having a nightmare, but he found him being suffocated by a long strand of white hair instead. The host cut the lock in half using a pair of scissors. In the morning, he found the man's white horse dead.

Marui, known as the kitchen demon, is another side of Marzanna. When she senses danger, the deity hides behind the stove of the person who should be alarmed. She twirls around, making scary, thumping noises. She transforms into a butterfly and enters the bedroom, attracting nightmares. Women used to say prayers when they needed to spin something. Otherwise, they believed that the deity would visit at night and ruin all their work.

Rituals and Celebrations

Slavs who still embrace folk and religious holidays celebrate the arrival of spring with the feast of Maslenitsa. This holiday is also held in commemoration of the dead, encouraging families to come together, join activities like sledding and sleigh rides, and have delicious food and drinks. Pancakes, crepes, cheese, and butter are among the most popular meals that people eat on Maslenitsa, the day before Lent begins, which involves abstaining from consuming dairy products for 40 days.

During the festival, a life-sized figurine of a maiden is made of straw and dressed in rags. The doll, which is a symbolic representation of the goddess Marzanna, is then carried through the fields and either burned or drowned in a body of water. Burning the straw maiden represents the act of getting rid of winter, and drowning the doll signifies the goddess' trip to the underworld.

Folklore

While the tale of Jarylo and Marzanna perfectly explains the rationale behind the changing seasons, at least two other folklore tales explain the cyclical nature of the seasons. One of these stories revolves around her relationship, as Morana, with Dazbog, the god of the sun, which is very similar to her tale with Jarylo.

Morana and Dazbog were initially lovers and established balance and harmony in the world. However, Dazbog left her for someone else, causing Morana to abandon her duty as the goddess of winter. The days became shorter and warmer, bringing the onset of spring. Morana, however, sought revenge and poisoned Dazbog, and winter returned harsher than it had ever before. Dazbog then banished Morana to the underworld, an event associated with the dormancy of winter. This caused spring, then eventually summer, to return.

Marzanna and the arrival of winter are also associated with the *Enchanted Huntsman* folktale. This tale is very similar to that of Persephone and Demeter, which explains the changing seasons, too. While Persephone, Demeter's daughter (the goddess of agriculture), was out picking flowers, Hades, the god of the underworld, was astounded by her beauty and kidnapped her. Demeter entered a dark state of grief, at which she abandoned her duties, and Earth withered. As a compromise, Hades agreed to send Persephone out from the underworld for a portion of every year. When Persephone comes out, spring and summer occur, and when she's in the underworld, fall and winter overtake the Earth.

Marzanna, in the aspect of Morana, seduced the huntsman, who happened to be the god of the sun. He was charmed by her beauty and fell in love with her. As Hades did to Persephone, Morana trapped the huntsman's soul, which symbolizes light, warmth, and summer, in a magic mirror representing the underworld. This cut the days short and led to the emergence of winter and its harsh weather conditions. According to this lore, spring only arises when Morana's sister Zhiva, the goddess of summer, arrives after Morana's symbolic burning and drowning rituals during Maslenista. This recurrent theme, whether with Jarylo and Marzanna, Persephone and Demeter, Morana and Dazbog, or Morana and the huntsman, shows how people around the world always tried to explain worldly phenomena through common archetypes.

Baba Yaga and Marzanna are two widely feared, dark, and powerful women in Slavic mythology. Reading their mythology, anyone would think that they're inherently evil villains. However, when you learn more about them, you come to learn that they're deeply misunderstood. Both figures open a window into the Slavic culture and show how people at that time and place attempted to make sense of the world around them.

Chapter 6: Hindu Goddesses

Hindus believe in one supreme god called Brahman. They are also polytheists and believe in the existence of multiple gods and goddesses who reflect aspects of Brahman characteristics.

This chapter provides a comprehensive and insightful exploration of the Hindu Dark Goddesses Kali/Kaalika, Durga, Chinnamasta, and Chamunda.

Hindu Goddesses.

Kali

Kali is usually depicted with blue skin.
https://commons.wikimedia.org/wiki/File:Kali_by_Raja_Ravi_Varma.jpg

Kali is depicted as a frightening figure with black or blue skin and four arms, wearing a skirt made of arms and a necklace made of skulls, with her tongue sticking out, and she is holding a knife covered in blood.

Mythology

Kali was the daughter of the war goddess Durga, who was a vicious warrior and a destructive force. Durga had ten arms and carried a weapon in each one. In one battle, she was fighting the buffalo demon, Mahishasura. She arrived riding a lion to frighten her enemies. However, it didn't work, as the demon was invincible. Durga was furious for failing to defeat him. Suddenly, something burst from her forehead. It was Kali, created from her mother's wrath, filled with bloodlust and a destructive nature. She devoured all the demons on the battlefield and wore their heads as a necklace.

However, Kali's violence didn't stop there. She attacked any deity or human who sinned or made a mistake. She was out of control, and neither the gods nor mankind knew what to do with her. Shiva, who was also her husband, had no choice but to intervene. He lay down on her path, and it was only when she stepped on him that she suddenly became ashamed for failing to recognize her husband and was then able to calm down.

In another birth myth, Parvati, the goddess of love, shed her skin and transformed into Kali.

In another version of her birth story, the mighty demon called Daruka was terrorizing mankind and the deities. According to legend, only a woman could kill him. The gods asked Parvati to save them and kill the demon. She transformed into Kali and put an end to Daruka.

In one last myth, a demon called Raktabija was causing trouble on Earth. Even the gods felt helpless and didn't know what to do with him. He was different from any other demon they met because he was able to make new demons with every drop of his blood. So attacking him was impossible.

The gods agreed to work together and create a super-being to defeat Raktabija, and this being was Kali. She devoured all the demons without spilling one drop of blood.

Kali wasn't a thoughtless and merciless murderer. In one myth, a group of thieves kidnapped a monk and were planning to kill him near her statue. Kali was enraged that they dared to harm a monk. Suddenly, her statue came to life, and she punished the thieves.

Key Characteristics

If you observe these stories, you will notice that Kali is a mother figure. She only killed demons to keep her people safe; she isn't a murderer but a protector.

Although she is recounted in an unattractive manner, she is described in many poems as voluptuous, young, and attractive, with a very nice smile, which many men find irresistible. She is a force of creation and is associated with traits of tantric creativity.

Popular Forms

- **Dhumavati:** an incarnation of Kali as a widow.
- **Kamala Kali:** goddess of prosperity and wealth.
- **Shodoshi:** a seductress form of Kali.
- **Tara:** known for her violence and blue color.
- **Bhairavi Kali:** a motherly figure and bringer of death.

- **Shamsana Kali:** a more human version of Kali with only two arms and no protruding tongue.

Symbolism

You probably think that Kali is a heartless murderer. However, the goddess only kills demons. She rarely ever hurts a human being or another deity. In fact, she liberated the souls of many innocent people and helped them to live better lives. Since Kali is also depicted naked, she has become a symbol of sexuality, nurturing, and purity. She is also sometimes shown with three eyes to symbolize omniscience.

Although most of the myths about Kali portray her as bloodthirsty, she is highly venerated and extremely popular among her people mainly because of her role as a tantric goddess. Tantric deities are a pantheon of goddesses who follow the rules and principles of Hinduism.

Duality

Kali represents the destructive aspect of the dark feminine, tearing down illusions and ego to pave the way for spiritual transformation. Even though she is associated with violence, Kali is a loving mother figure who represents fertility, creativity, and feminine energy. Her duality plays a big role in her symbolism. She is a terrifying figure who could kill mercilessly, yet she also represents the metaphysical affairs associated with death.

Her four arms perfectly reflect her duality. She holds a demon's head and a sword in two hands and blesses her followers with the others.

Dark Feminine

Kali's appearance is different from any other deity. Her features are fierce and terrifying. She rules over death, doomsday, destruction, and time. She is also the goddess of violence, sexuality, and motherly love. It is believed that Kali is the incarnation of Parvati, the Hindu god Shiva's wife. "Kali" means "she who is death" or "she who is black."

Archetype

Kali symbolizes protection and love. She connects her worshipers to their emotions, strength, and power. She motivates you to be committed, passionate, and alive. She is the archetype of wild women who are in touch with their instincts and emotions.

Worship/Rituals

Instructions:

1. Find a picture of Kali.
2. Sit in a quiet place with no distractions.
3. Light a white candle and take a few deep breaths.
4. Repeat "I am safe and protected" three times.
5. Think of everything that has been upsetting you lately, and focus on them for two to five minutes.
6. Open your eyes and focus on Kali's pictures.
7. Take in every detail and say what you notice either in your mind or out loud.
8. Only focus on Kali and repeat her name out loud for three minutes.
9. Close your eyes and invoke Kali. Ask her energy to flow through you.
10. Spend a few minutes with her, then thank her.

Durga

Durga is also called Devi or Shakti.

https://commons.wikimedia.org/wiki/File:Durga_Mahisasuramardini.JPG

Durga is also called Devi or Shakti. She is the mother of the universe and protector of all mankind and deities. She is one of the most significant and popular goddesses in Hinduism. She represents harmony and everything good in the universe.

Mythology

The buffalo demon, Mahishasura, was terrorizing the world, and the gods tried to capture him but failed. So Shiva, the Supreme Being, and the destroyer, Brahma, the creator, and Vishnu, the god of preservation, created Durga to kill the demon. She was a beautiful, strong, brave, and fierce warrior. No one could ever defeat her. She was created as a grown woman ready to fight. She fought Mahishasura viciously and slayed him while he was transforming into a buffalo.

Durga fought many demons and protected the world from destruction and bloodshed on multiple occasions. Many of these demons represented negative qualities like anger, arrogance, hypocrisy, pride, and greed. So Durga was also protecting the human soul and fighting evil forces so people would live in harmony with one another.

Key Characteristics

Durga is a Sanskrit word meaning "fort." Her name reflects her militant and protective nature. She is also called "Durgatinashini," meaning "the one eliminating all sufferings." She is shown as a woman with eight arms, so she is always prepared to fight her enemies from every direction.

She is called Tryambake, meaning "the three-eyed goddess." Her right eye is the sun, and it represents action; her left eye is the moon and symbolizes desire. Her middle eye is fire and represents knowledge.

She is the goddess of strength and war and is illustrated riding a lion and holding weapons.

Popular Forms

Durga has multiple incarnations:

- Kali
- Bhagvati
- Bhavani
- Ambika
- Lalita
- Gauri
- Kundalini

• Java

Rajeswari When she appeared as herself, she would manifest into any of these nine deities:

- Skandamata
- Kusumanda
- Shailaputri
- Kaalratri
- Brahmacharini
- Maha Gauri
- Katyayani
- Chandraghanta
- Siddhidatri

Symbolism

Durga has multiple weapons, and each symbolizes an aspect of her personality.

- **Sword:** A symbol of truth and knowledge.
- **Trident:** Healing spiritual, mental, and physical suffering.
- **A budding lotus flower:** Unaccomplished triumph since the battle of good vs. evil is eternal.
- **Thunderbolt:** Strong beliefs in a person's convictions.
- **Bow and arrow:** Her protective abilities and power.
- **Conch shell:** Her connection to the Divine.

Duality

Dugra may seem more like a destructive weapon than a goddess. However, she has a compassionate side hidden behind her tough and scary exterior. Her only purpose is protecting mankind from the demons who want to bring their downfall.

Dark Feminine

Durga is a mother goddess with powerful divine femininity. She is creative, nurturing, and protective. Although she is a fierce warrior, she isn't driven by bloodlust. She fights her battles with focus, mastery, and composure. She courageously confronts demons and comes out victorious.

Archetype

Durga represents the female archetype for one's inner and outer power. She pushes you to set boundaries to protect your energy from negative people.

Worship/Rituals

- Offer her flowers to show your devotion.
- Light a candle near her idol.
- Chant "Om Aim Hreem Kleem Chamundaye Vichche" to get rid of bad luck, health problems, and negative energy.

Chinnamasta

Chinnamasta is a tantric goddess.

https://commons.wikimedia.org/wiki/File:Chinnamasta_above_Kama_and_Rati_on_a_lotus_flower_-_18th_century_Nepalese_painting.jpg

Chinnamasta is a tantric goddess. She is an incarnation of the love goddess Parvati. Her name is derived from two Sanskrit words, "Chhinna," meaning severed, and "Masta" meaning head. So the name means "the one with the severed head."

Mythology

One day, Parvati and her attendants went to take a bath at the Mandakini River. Suddenly, for some mysterious reason, Parvati was aroused, and her color changed to black. At the same time, for unknown reasons, her attendants also got very hungry and demanded to be fed right away. Since she was a motherly figure, she couldn't see them suffering. She made the ultimate sacrifice and severed her head with a sword.

Blood streams were coming out of her neck, which she used to feed her attendants. After they were full, she placed her head back in its place.

Another myth about Chinnamasta's birth is similar to Kali's and Durga's story. There was a war between demons and gods. The gods were outnumbered, and the demons were too strong for them. So they asked the goddess Mahashakti for assistance. She fought the demons and killed them, then she severed her head to drink her blood.

Key Characteristics

Chinnamasta is depicted holding her severed head in her left hand and a sword in her right hand. In other illustrations, she is depicted with four arms, naked, wearing ornaments and a skull garland. The severed head is usually drinking blood coming out of her neck.

She represents sexual desires, life, death, and self-control, and she is the supreme goddess, the mother of the universe, and the goddess of transformation and feminine energy.

Popular Forms

- Indrani, goddess of wrath and jealousy
- Bhairavi, goddess of decay
- Varnini, an attendant
- Dhakini, the sky dweller
- Vajravairochani is another name for Chinnamasta
- Chanda Prachandi Devi, the demon destroyer

Symbolism

- Chinnamasta has a serpent around her neck, which represents power.
- Her naked body is a symbol of worldly things and abandonment.
- Severing her head symbolizes letting go of her ego.

- She is depicted standing over two dead bodies, reflecting her control over her sexual desires.

Duality

Chinnamasta's scary image is completely different from her caring and compassionate nature. Cutting her head off may seem psychotic to some people, but she did it out of love and devotion to feed her attendants. She only fights demons to protect mankind.

Dark Feminine

Chinnamasta is a symbol of sacrifice, courage, and feminine power.

Archetype

Chinnamasta is an archetype of your subconscious, and tapping into it to come up with loving changing ideas.

Worship/Rituals

Valediction to Chinnamasta

Instructions:

1. Get a statue of Chinnamasta.
2. Light a scented candle as an offering to the goddess.
3. Ask her for forgiveness, then make an offering and place it at her feet.
4. Fill a conch shell with water.
5. Sprinkle it on yourself to gain her blessings.

Chamunda

Chamunda is associated with Shiva.
https://commons.wikimedia.org/wiki/File:Chamunda_Dancing_-_1700.jpg

Before Chamunda joined the Hindu pantheon, she was worshiped by different tribes. Chamunda is associated with Shiva. She is the only goddess to emerge from the energy of the supreme goddess since all the gods that came before her were males. She stands out for having a different appearance and weapons.

Mythology

There were once two demon brothers called Shumbha and Nishumbha. They were extremely ambitious and wanted to take over the world. So they hid in a temple and tortured themselves for thousands of years. Their actions impressed Brahma, the creator, who told them they could have any reward they wanted. They asked that no man nor male god would have any power over them. This made them immortal, as no one could ever hurt or kill them.

They became powerful enough to execute their plan and conquer the world. The gods weren't pleased with the demons' growing power, so the goddess Devi Parvati decided to put an end to them. She resided in a place near the demons, hoping that they or their attendants would notice her. Her plan worked, and because of her exquisite beauty, she caught the attention of one of the attendants.

He told Shumbha about her, and Shumbha asked for her to be brought to his court right away. However, Devi Parvati refused, which angered the demon brothers. They commanded their attendants to bring her by force. They were worried that someone was supporting her and turning her against them.

Their attendants tried for one last time to ask her nicely to join the demons, but she still refused. They were tired of her and decided to kidnap her and take her to Shumbha. When they tried to catch her, she roared at them so loudly they were turned to ashes. She sent her lion after their army of demons, and they devoured them.

Shumbha and Nishumbha were furious and sent a huge army after her, led by demons Chanda and Munda. When Devi Parvati saw the army approaching, Chandika Jayasundara emerged from her forehead and defeated them, killing Chanda and Munda. Devi Parvati then drank their blood and danced to celebrate her victory. She called her Chamunda, a contraction of Chanda and Munda, for her brave and fearless victory.

Key Characteristics

Chamunda is the goddess of nature, war, famine, and disasters, and she is the chief yogini, a group of Tantric gods who act as devi Pavarti attendants. She is portrayed as having three eyes, four arms, red skin, and thick red hair decorated with a crescent moon and skulls.

Popular Forms

Chamunda has eight different forms. She is one of the Saptamatrikas, seven mother goddesses.

Symbolism

Chamunda's fierce features reflect her strength and power against her enemies and how she protects her worshipers from evil. The skull necklace represents life's cycle, which ends in death.

Duality

Chamunda may be one of the most frightening deities in Hinduism, but she is compassionate, loving, a mother figure, and a protector to all her worshipers. People pray to her to protect them, fight demons and evil powers, and to also provide guidance and strength.

Dark Feminine

Chamunda is the female energy of the god of death, Yama. She is a terrifying figure who brings famine, disasters, and epidemics.

Archetype

Chamunda's archetype is also the subconscious mind, as she helps you tap into this part of yourself to discover who you truly are.

Worship/Rituals

Instructions:

1. Find a room with no distractions.
2. Place crystals like rose quartz and citrine on the floor to make a circle.
3. Sit in a comfortable position in the circle.
4. Call on your ancestors, spirit guides, or guardian angels for assistance.
5. Take five long and deep breaths.
6. Make an offering to the goddess, like wine.
7. Focus on what you are feeling right now.
8. Set an intention to let go of anything holding you back, either by thinking about it or by chanting, "Let it go."
9. Repeat Chamunda's mantra on a bead: "Om Eim Hrim Kilm Chamundayei Vechei Namaha," meaning "Om and salutations to

the radiant one who has wisdom and power."

10. Lie down and take a few deep breaths so you can absorb the energy.

11. Express your gratitude to Chamunda and all the spirits who assisted you in your ritual.

Looking at the pictures of any of these Hindu goddesses can give you nightmares. However, you shouldn't judge them by their appearance. They can be killers, and sometimes their anger gets out of control, but they never harm a human being, and their instinct is to always protect. They are all mother figures who were willing to do anything to keep their children (worshipers) safe.

Remember to be respectful when you call on them and express your gratitude after every ritual. You don't want to get on their bad side. Live by the morals they represent and be kind, caring, and compassionate. Don't be in a rush to establish a connection with them, and understand that these things take time.

Chapter 7: African Goddesses

Many people are familiar with Norse, Greek, and ancient Egyptian mythologies. Their gods and goddesses are usually featured in movies, TV shows, and literature. Who doesn't know the Norse God Thor, the Greek Goddess Aphrodite, or the Egyptian Goddess Cleopatra? However, there is an equally fascinating and enchanting mythology that doesn't get the same attention: ancient African mythology. Many gods and goddesses in Africa deserve the same recognition as their Western counterparts.

This chapter focuses on the Dark Goddesses in African mythology.

African Goddess.

Oya

Oya, the goddess of magic and graveyards.

Oya is a goddess worshiped in many African traditions, such as Yoruba and Santeria. However, she isn't usually referred to as a goddess but as an Orisha. This is a term that describes supernatural beings or deities that help mankind and act as intermediaries between them and the supreme god, Oldumare.

Oya is a fierce goddess who rules over the winds and storms. She can either bring a gentle breeze on a hot summer day or a hurricane destroying everything in her way. However, Oya has a much darker side as the guardian of the cemeteries and the dead. She watches over graveyards and protects the spirits. She exists in the realm of the living and the dead and can easily travel between both worlds. Oya shares a unique bond with the spirits of the departed, and she accompanies them to the other world where they will spend their eternity.

Origin

Oya originates from the African religion Yoruba. Her name is derived from the African phrase "O Ya," meaning "she tore," which refers to her explosive nature. She is the daughter of Obatala, the Orisha of mankind and compassion, and Yemaya, the mother of all Orishas.

Mythology

In Yoruba mythology, Oya was a human being who had great powers. She was a fierce warrior who protected the weak, especially women. She also liberated many enslaved people in the Yoruba revolution. Since Oya didn't live an ordinary life, she was gifted with an extraordinary destiny after she died and became an Orisha.

She was married to the Orisha of thunder, Shango. He was also married to two other Orishas, Oba and Oshun, who were also Oya's sisters. Interestingly, Shango was also their brother. Oya was his favorite wife, and they had a passionate relationship. They were madly in love and one of the strongest couple deities in Yoruba.

Sadly, Oya didn't have any children sired by her husband. She got pregnant nine times, but none of her children survived birth. She kept their memory alive by wearing nine-colored scarves around her waist. In another legend, she made a sacrifice by offering a sacred piece of cloth, and she was blessed with four sets of twins and a ninth child. For this reason, she is called "The mother of nine."

Attributes

Oya is a brave, courageous, and powerful warrior. She is shown as a beautiful and strong black woman carrying a sword in one hand to bring change and cut through any obstacles her followers may face. On the other hand, she is holding a fan to control storms and winds.

Oya is associated with destruction, transformation, and change. She can control earthquakes, tornadoes, winds, storms, and lighting. She is also the Orisha of clairvoyance, intuition, and rebirth. She is very wise, and women call on her when facing a conflict they can't resolve on their own.

People love and fear Oya. She is a fierce protector and a loving mother to all her followers. However, when she gets angry, she destroys homes and lands, bringing much suffering to her people. She appreciates honesty and justice and can't tolerate lies and deceit.

Oya can also heal. People call on her when their life is out of balance or after the death of a loved one. She is also the goddess of fertility and protector of crops.

Oya has a very famous dance that can either bring gentle wind or violence and chaos. It depends on her mood.

She also rules over the marketplace and keeps her eyes open for con artists and thieves. Merchants and traders usually pray to her before they embark on a business endeavor.

Cultural Significance

Although Oya originated in the Yoruba religion, her cultural significance extends to other cultures and traditions. In the Brazilian Candomblé, Oya represents compassion, and she is the protector of all women. In the Cuban religion, Santeria, she represents the modern woman who defies social norms. This shows that Oya is a universal Orisha who embodies various aspects that resonate with people from different cultures.

Oya's cultural significance is shown in literature, music, and art. For instance, she was featured in Nigerian writer Chinua Achebe's poems.

Symbols

In one African legend, Oya had a black ram who was a loyal and trusted friend. However, he turned against her and tried to kill her. She was heartbroken over this betrayal and swore to never trust a ram again. Since then, female goats have become one of her symbols.

Other symbols:

- Iruke
- Machete
- Marketplace
- Cemetery
- Fire
- Thunderbolt
- Wind
- Niger River
- Number nine
- Guinea hen
- Buffalo
- Plums
- Amber
- Violet
- Musk

- Dark chocolate
- Ruby
- Moonstone
- Amber
- Burgundy
- Purple
- Brown

Oya, the Dark Goddess

As the Orisha of new life and rebirth, Oya is considered a Dark Goddess because of her association with death and cemeteries. She guides people away from the darkness and into the light, giving them hope after turmoil. Oya travels between the realms of the living and the dead. She has the power of life and death. She can keep the dead on Earth if they have unfinished business. She can also bring the dead to her whenever she wants. This is why she is called the "Great Mother of Witches (Elders of the Night)."

After a person dies, Oya must take their spirit immediately to the afterlife to keep both realms in order and prevent the dead from roaming around aimlessly among the living. In a way, she protects the living as well from the fear of watching spirits walking around them.

Rituals/Worship

Worshiping any goddess requires making offerings. Oya loves eggplants, plums, female goat meat, guinea hen meat, pigeon meat, black hen meat, dark chocolate, and red wine.

You can also pray to her when you are experiencing change. If your life is turning upside down, ask Oya to bless you with stability and reassurance. She can take away the negative energy that is disturbing your life.

If you want to communicate with your ancestors, call on Oya. Since she stands between the realm of the living and the realm of the dead, she can deliver your messages to your loved ones.

If you or someone requires healing, hold an egg and pray to Oya to remove the negative energy making them sick. Then, crack the egg in a glass of water to release the negativity.

If Oya is calling on you, she will bring sudden changes in your life to push you toward growth and transformation. She may also appear to you in dreams or send you one of her symbols, like storms or lighting. She is trying to communicate with you if you find yourself drawn toward her mythology or symbols.

Invoking Oya:

1. Set up an altar during a wind, lightning, rain, or storm.
2. Add any of her symbols or her picture to the altar.
3. Light a purple or any dark-colored candles.
4. Make an offering.
5. Write your intention on a piece of paper.
6. Sit near the altar in a comfortable position and close your eyes.
7. Clear your mind and focus on your breathing.
8. Visualize Oya and ask for her guidance or to communicate with a departed loved one.
9. Pay attention to what you may see or feel during the meditation.
10. After you finish, express your gratitude to her.

Yewa

Yewa is one of the most mysterious Orishas. She is Oya's sister and lives with her in graveyards among the dead. She also rules over cemeteries and prevents the spirits from roaming among the living. She is the Orisha of death, loneliness, chastity, virgins, and fertility. However, she doesn't cause death. She just helps the spirits reach their final resting place. She receives the spirits of the dead and takes them to Oya, who escorts them to the afterlife.

Origins

Yewa originated from the Yoruba religion. Her name is derived from the words "Yeye," meaning mother, and "Awa," meaning our, so she is often referred to as "Our mother." She used to be a patron for women and mothers. Her story is unclear. In one version, she was never a mother because she was never married and was a virgin. She did, however, become the protector and goddess of all virgins.

Mythology

Yewa wasn't always a dark Orisha who lived in the graves. Her life was completely different. She was a young and naive virgin who was known for her beauty and chastity. Every male Orisha had eyes on her and wanted to possess her. One of these Orishas was Shango, a famous womanizer who seduced many female Orishas. When he saw Yewa, he became infatuated with her and started chasing her.

He seduced her, and the innocent girl had no idea of Shango's intentions. She got pregnant and hoped he would be by her side and support her. However, he disappeared, leaving her all alone. Yewa was humiliated and felt used, desperate, and scared. She then lost her child and buried it under a tree. This experience left her traumatized, and she retreated to the cemeteries to live with her sister.

When Olokun, the Orisha at the bottom of the ocean, learned about what happened to her, he went to the tree and brought back her unborn child to life. He named him Borosia, and he became Olokun's guard.

The rest of the story remains unclear. In one version, she married Boromu, the Orisha of the desert and guardian of the cemetery and human bones. Boromu was in love with her, but he may also have wanted to protect her honor. In another version, she continued living in the cemetery.

There is another less tragic version of Yewa's story. Yewa took a vow of chastity and hid away from temptation in her father's Obatala castle. When Shango heard about the beautiful virgin, he decided he must have her. When he reached the castle and saw her, he was mesmerized by her beauty. Yewa also felt a strong attraction to Shango, and her feelings confused and scared her.

She went to her father and sought his guidance. Obatala loved his daughter, but he understood that she must be protected from these lustful feelings. So he sent her to the realm of the dead to guard over the cemeteries. No man or Orisha could ever come close to that realm, so no one could tempt or distract her from her vow.

Attributes

Yewa is depicted as a beautiful and skinny woman dressed in pink who can transform into an owl. She was originally a water spirit, but she then became a virgin goddess of decorum, reclusiveness, and morality. She is a guardian of the innocent, but if you disrespect her, she will bring suffering and pain.

She is extremely diligent, wise, intelligent, strong-willed, sweet, and knowledgeable. Yewa is a mother figure and an archetype of chastity. Orula, the Orisha of oracles and wisdom, bestowed on her the power of clairvoyance. Yewa rules over the cosmos and the night skies. She can transform water into gas to create clouds and rain. She is associated with the darkness, where spirits find themselves after they leave their human form.

Cultural Significance

Yewa originated in Nigeria. She is highly revered in Africa and was the Orisha of the Yewa River. In Yoruba, Candomblé, and Santeria, Yewa is the Orisha of death. She was first an Orisha of birth, fertility, and water. Then, she became responsible for separating the realm of the dead from the living. This change took place during the slave trade. When enslaved people arrived in South America, they established a religion derived from Yoruba called Santeria, where Yewa was the Orisha of death. After her marriage to Boromu, she became associated with death like her husband.

In Cuba, she is also the Orisha of death and rules over the cemeteries, and she also represents purity and virginity.

Symbols

- Any body of water like ponds, lakes, or rivers.
- Pink veils
- Gravestones
- Fridays
- Owls
- Seashells
- Dolphins
- Fish
- White lotus (represents innocence and purity.)
- Meadowsweet flowers
- Orchids
- Chrysanthemums
- Lilies
- Flowers
- Scents like apricot, water lily, bergamot, vanilla, rose, orange, and mint.
- Pearls
- Pink
- Number 11

Yewa, the Dark Goddess

Yewa is the guardian of the graveyards. She dances over people's tombs to bring peace to their souls and let them know she is here guarding and protecting them. However, she still protects the innocent, pure, and virgins. If someone tries to harm them, she makes them suffer.

Yewa believes that the dead should be respected. So if someone mocks them or desecrates their graves, she will bring her wrath down on them.

Rituals/Worship

To properly worship Yewa and avoid her wrath, never swear in front of her altar or image. Since she is a virgin, refrain from offending her by talking about sex, having sex, or making sexual innuendos near her altar. Respect all people and never start a fight with anyone.

If Yewa is calling you, you will experience spiritual purity and a desire to be alone. You will also be more interested in introspection or meditation. Yewa may also come to you in dreams, either as herself or sending you one of her symbols like a cemetery or a skull.

Make offerings to Yewa such as white guinea fowl meat, white pigeon meat, white hen meat, goat meat, and herbs like fennel, cypress, and tua.

Invoking Yewa:

1. Find a quiet place.
2. Build an altar and add any symbols of her or her pictures.
3. Light black or burgundy candles.
4. Make an offering like flowers or fish.
5. Write down your intention on a piece of paper, then place it on the altar.
6. Sit in a comfortable position and close your eyes.
7. Take a few deep breaths.
8. Visualize Yewa and ask for her guidance.
9. Express your gratitude after you have finished.

Ala

Ala is a goddess from the Odinala tradition that originated in South Nigeria. Odinala holds women in very high regard and even puts them ahead of men. Ala is called "The mother of all things," and she is present at the beginning and end of one's life.

Origins

Ala is an Igbo word meaning "ground." Her mother is the goddess of fertility for animals and humans, guardian of the harvest, ruler of the underworld, and the goddess of the earth, and her father is the great god Chuku.

Mythology

In Ibo regions, Ala is worshiped in square-shaped homes called "Mbari." Inside, there are large, bright-colored statues of Ala. She usually sends a bee nest or a snake to the location where she wants her followers to build a Mbari. Men and women who help build this sacred structure feel honored and connected to the goddess.

Attributes

She is the goddess of death, cleansing, joy, luck, creativity, and morality. She is the Earth mother, guardian of fertility, ruler of the underworld, and guardian of the harvest.

She has the power to make a child grow in their mother's womb. After birth, she stays with the child to guide and protect them until they reach adulthood. She also represents the four seasons.

Ala teaches people how to live honestly by emphasizing values like honor and loyalty. She is associated with morality, makes laws for the Igbo people to live by, and judges their actions. These laws are called Omenala, and if one breaks them, it is a great insult to Ala.

She is usually depicted carrying a small child since she is the protector of children and women.

Cultural Significance.

Ala is highly revered among the Igbo people. She is one of their main deities, and they live by her rules.

Symbols

- Yams
- Crescent moon
- Ants
- Python

Ala, the Dark Goddess

She is the underworld queen, and when a person dies, she takes their spirit into her womb so they can rest in peace. She has an army of ants to punish those who break her laws. They first appear in nightmares as a warning so you can make things right. Her army will bring severe punishment and suffering if you don't return to the right path.

Rituals/Worship

There are different ways to worship Ala. Light a candle when you wake up every morning to welcome her. You can also make an offering of yam since it is her favorite food.

The best time to worship Ala is during the spring. Build an altar, add her pictures and symbols, and light a candle.

African Dark Goddesses are strong and fierce and must be respected. Although they have dark aspects, they keep the realm of the living safe and in order by taking the souls of the dead to the afterlife. They care about the spirits either by keeping them safe like Ala, who keeps them in her womb, or by keeping them company like Yewa, who dances on their graves.

They also serve the living by providing guidance and taking them from the darkness to the light. Always appease the Dark Goddess because they have a bad temper.

Chapter 8: Celtic/Irish Goddesses

People often hear the terms Celtic and Irish Mythology used interchangeably, begging the question of whether or not they are one and the same. The answer is __no__.

Irish mythology is similar to Celtic mythology, like *Protestantism* is to *Christianity*, one branch of a big tree. The pre-Christian beliefs of the Celtics housed the tales of the Scots, Irish, and Brittonics. Olden myths and rituals were passed down the generations through word of mouth. Of the three main branches, the Irish stories are the best preserved, thanks to the efforts made by the Christian monks who wove the tales into the historical records during the Middle Ages.

In most theologies, ancient deities were patrons for more than one realm and were seen as protectors of acts like love, fertility, and land. Often, they shared the responsibilities of the realms with other gods, making it hard to distinguish the specific roles of each one of them.

The Celtic and Irish mythologies have an enigmatic ambiance to them. Home to many magical and other-worldly beings whose tales can keep you on the edge of your seat.

As you make your way through the chapter, you'll find yourself engrossed in the world of the dark and powerful deities that the ancestors revered and feared at the same time.

The Morrigan

She is one of the most prominent and fierce figures in Celtic History; a formidable warrior, unchallenged by anyone, avidly worshiped despite her ferociousness, beauty, and brutality.

Who Is She?

The great queen goddess represented war, fate, and death. She was also a gifted shapeshifter, with her most common transformation being into a raven. She would often appear before battles in her raven form, either terrifying or inspiring the soldiers to fight harder. In some other tales, she would appear as a wolf or an eel. She sometimes employed her shapeshifting skills to transform into a beautiful woman so she could seduce powerful men. More tales show the goddess depicted as an old ugly hag.

Her name often changed with whomever was telling the story. She was referred to as the Celtic goddess of death, Morrigu, or the queen of the triple goddesses, among many other names.

Her name is a subject of controversy among scholars. Some say that the first part of her name, "Mor," is interpreted in old Irish as the word phantom. Others are convinced that it is linked to the Anglo-Saxon word "maere," which translates to nightmare or death. At times, people spelled the word "Mor" with an accent on the O, turning its meaning into great.

The other half of her name, "Rigan," means queen and corresponds with the Latin word Regina, meaning great queen. Put together, you've got "great queen" or "Phantom Queen" to add to the list of names she had.

In the old scriptures, it was assumed that she could foresee the death of warriors in battle, often influencing the outcome of the conflict.

In some Irish tales, she was addressed as one of the three war goddesses, along with her other two sisters, Macha and Neman or (Badb). In others, she was represented as both an individual and three distinct personalities under a single name. Those tales sometimes referred to Macha, Badb, and Neman as the Morrigan. Other tales are named Danu or Anand instead of Neman. These discrepancies cast a shadow on the truth of how the goddess was seen through the eyes of the ancient Celtics. When she's viewed as three goddesses the Morrigan gains more powers than when she stands alone. On her own, she is the great goddess of war and death, while with her sisters, she becomes the guardian of land, goddess of fertility, and a sovereignty goddess.

The Morrigan can easily be compared with the Norse Valkyries, the Furies, and Kali of Hindu mythology, goddess of destruction and transformation. So, in a nutshell, the Morrigan is heavily linked to carnage, war, and blood.

Her Symbols

The Morrigan is associated with more than one symbol in the Celtic/Irish Mythology. The symbol would change depending on the version of the story being told and the perspective from which it's recited.

1. Ravens

In most stories, at the mention of a raven, thoughts immediately go to death and the end of life since the birds are often seen after battles picking at the remains of the dead. They also symbolized witchcraft and magic, which is a common association even today. Since the goddess often chose to take the form of the raven, specifically in battle, it made sense that it would be one of her symbols.

2. The Moon

This representation has something to do with the goddess having a triple nature. The ancestors considered the moon's changing phases between waxing, waning, and full as a heavenly cycle. Also, as it continuously changes its shape throughout the month, it reminds the people of the goddess' ability to shapeshift herself.

3. The Triskelion

In the old days, this symbol was considered one of the main signs of divinity, coincidentally also signifying the number three. It made sense to attribute it to the Morrigan since she was made up of three goddesses in some beliefs.

The Family Tree

In Irish folklore, the goddess is said to be one of the three daughters (a variation of those sisters was Badb, Anann, and Macha) of the Irish goddess and sorceress Ernmas. It was said that she was the wife of the god Dagda. There are two versions about her origin and when exactly she came to be. The Tuatha de Danann places the mother and daughter with the tribe of supernatural and mythical beings and associates them with the goddess Danu. In this version of the tale, the Morrigan is believed to have fought alongside her sisters in the battle against the Fomorions and the Firbolg, using magic to win the fight and gain a foothold in Ireland.

In the Ulster Cycle, which some believe precedes the Tuatha de Danann, the Morrigan is said to have existed in the copper age in 3000 BCE. However, not much evidence supports this theory. In her early depictions in Irish literature, she was referred to as "Monster in the form of a Woman" and "Ominous Creature," which gives you an idea of why she was consistently linked to death.

Her role in death consisted of prophesying and influencing it at times. Her other two sisters completed the cycle, with each one representing a different characteristic of the relationship between life and death.

The Morrigan and Cu Chulainn

One of the well-known stories of the Morrigan involves the Celtic Hero Cu Chulainn. It is said that the warrior was following a stray heifer that he'd lost. In his mind, the heifer had been stolen and placed in another location. He found it in the same territory where the Morrigan happened to be at the same time.

The young man started attacking the Morrigan with sharp language, accusing her of the theft without knowing that he was in the presence of a deity. The goddess then turned herself into a raven and landed on a branch near him. The warrior immediately backtracked and asked for forgiveness, for he would have never disrespected the goddess had he known who she was. The Morrigan then proceeded to accuse him of touching her in his rage, which infuriated the warrior, sending him into another offensive tirade at the goddess. Instead of exacting divine vengeance then and there, the Morrigan warned the warrior that he would die in the coming battle, and she would be there to witness his demise.

The day of battle came. The warrior was in a fight with Queen Maeve (also known as Med), attempting to defend the province of Ulster from her invasion. Out of nowhere, a fair maiden happened upon him. The beautiful woman offered herself to the hero but was promptly rejected. The young beauty turned out to be the Morrigan. Furious at the way she had been treated, she turned herself into an eel and attempted to attack Cu Chulainn as he was crossing a fjord. The young warrior fought back and injured the animal.

Adamant to restore her wounded pride, the goddess then changed into a wolf and went after the hero, charging a herd of cattle in an attempt to trample him under their feet. Cu Chulainn then used his slingshot to aim at the beast's eye, firing a stone and temporarily blinding the predator.

The goddess was not one to admit defeat, and she then changed form into a cow. In that form, she was able to inflame the rest of the herd, urging them to stampede toward the warrior.

The brave and cunning warrior managed to evade the herd and shoot yet another stone at the goddess's leg, breaking it immediately and forcing her to retreat.

After triumphing in battle against both Queen Maeve and the Morrigan, Cu Chulainn made his way back to his base, exhausted, seeking company and refuge. Along the way back, he met an old woman milking a cow. The warrior was too tired to notice that the old hag had similar injuries to the ones he had inflicted on the animals who attacked him. A blind eye and an injured leg.

Unable to assess the situation properly, Cu Chulainn stopped to chat with the old woman, who offered him milk to quench his thirst. The young man accepted the gesture, drank the milk, and blessed the old woman for her kindness. Upon doing so, unbeknownst to him, he restored the mighty goddess to her full strength.

The goddess was satisfied with her trickery of the warrior and did not attempt to engage in another fight with him.

It is said that the pair met once again before another one of Cu Chulainn's battles. On his way to the fight, he came upon a woman scrubbing blood off a suit of armor, which was considered a dark omen to see before a battle. He passed the woman and continued on his way. During the battle, he was fatally wounded. Using what was left of his strength, he tied himself to a boulder in an upright position to frighten any further oncoming enemies. A crow then settled on his shoulder, and he went into a deep sleep, never to wake again.

Macha

Macha is renowned for her powerful magic and need for vengeance.
https://commons.wikimedia.org/wiki/File:Macha.jpg

One of the goddesses thought to be a part of the Morrigan in certain myths is Macha. On the other hand, she was an individual member of the Tuatha de Danann, renowned for her powerful magic and voracious need for vengeance. She was rumored to have lived in Emain Macha's old fort.

She was the goddess of kinship, fire, fertility, land, horses, and warfare. Like the Morrigan, Macha was seen as a death omen who materialized as an apparition to warn people of impending doom.

Macha was revered as the big Mother Earth, the ultimate female, and the murderer of men. She was also known by several other names, such as Dana and Badb (crow or raven). Her name translated to "field" or "land plain." She was closely linked to the images of crows, acorns, and horses. Her three main attributes were her sexual fertility, her rural upbringing, and her maternal reproductive ability.

Macha is best known through five famous tales:

1. Partholon's Daughter

In the Leabhar Gabhala, she is referred to as the daughter of Partholon. In ancient legend, the Patholonians were among the second wave of settlers that came to Ireland. Some claim they were descendants of Noah. However, it is believed that they succumbed to a plague. Her reference in this tale is not prominent, and some believe that she was only included as an attempt by Christian monks to Christianize her.

2. Member of the Tuatha De Danann

In this tale, like her sister, the Morrigan, Macha is the daughter of Ernmas and Delbeath. She is depicted as the goddess of battle and war who used her magic to bring forth rain, fog, blood, and fire upon her enemies. It is believed that she may have fallen alongside King Nuada at the hands of Balor of the Baleful Eye at the battle of Moytura.

3. Nemed's Wife

In another tale, it is stated that she came along with the third wave of settlers to Ireland with her husband, Nemed. In this story, she doesn't last long, for she dies while cleaning out the land to plant it. She is portrayed as the goddess of fertility and land. Her grave is thought to be in a place called Ard Mhacha (meaning Macha's Height), known today as Armagh.

4. Wife of Cruinniuc

In the Ulster Cycle, she is seen as a fairy woman married to a wealthy farmer, Cruinniuc. She bears two children, twins. Macha had warned her husband not to mention her to anyone. During a festival held by the king of Ulster, attended by her husband, he overheard the king bragging about his horses and how fast they were. Unable to contain himself, Cruinniuc declared to the king that his wife could easily outrun any of his horses. Enraged by the insolence of the farmer, the king commanded him to bring forth his wife.

At the time, Macha was in labor and pleaded that the race be postponed. However, the king insisted, and she raced anyway. Macha succeeded in winning the race but at a high cost. She fell to the ground at the finish line, giving birth to her babies. Overcome with pain and anger, she cursed the men of Ulster, condemning them to suffer nine days of labor pain at the time of their greatest need and peril. The curse was to last for nine generations. As her children were brought to life, she was taken from it.

5. Macha of the Red Hair (Macha Mhongruadh)

Historians state that in this story, she is believed to have been the daughter of King Aodh Ruadh. The king was known to take turns ruling Ireland with two other kings. Each king was to rule for seven years. After the king's death following his third round, Macha demanded to take his place in the cycle as dictated by her birthright. Needless to say, the other two kings (Díthorba and Cimbáeth) had no interest in ruling with a woman.

They went into battle over the throne, and Macha was victorious, killing Dithorba in the process. After her seven years of ruling concluded, she was challenged by Dithorba's five sons. Macha informed them that she would allow them to battle for sovereignty. They accepted the challenge, and once again, she won. The five sons fled into the wild, and Macha married Cimbaeth to cement her claim to the throne so they could rule together.

The goddess then pursued the five sons alone, disguising herself in the form of a leper. One by one, she seduced and captured them. She then brought them home and forced them to build the fort of Emain Macha.

She ruled the land by her husband's side for seven years until he died, and then she continued to rule for another fourteen by herself until she was killed by Rechtaid Rigderg.

Badb

Badb is one of the goddesses believed to make up the triad of the Morrigan. She was known in the old days as the battle crow. It was common knowledge among worshipers that she played a role in gathering the souls of the fallen in battle and escorting them into the afterlife.

One of the forms she took was that of a petrifying woman who spreads fear and chaos. The goddess was linked to war, transformation, and a dominating presence that was awe-inspiring to mortals.

Her symbolism included the colors red and white (red clothes and white hair), which represent death in Celtic folklore. She was seen mostly as an old woman with one eye closed, standing on one foot, indicating the connection between the world of the living and the hereafter. She was also represented by crows and wolves, which symbolized guidance and transformation.

The Cauldron of Rebirth

Her name translates to "the one who boils," as she is seen in some illustrations tending to a magical cauldron in the other world. It was believed that when a warrior died in battle, they would see the goddess in the form of an old, kind woman stirring a cauldron. On meeting the goddess, the deceased warrior is asked whether they wish to stay or be reborn. If they chose to be reborn, they were then required to climb into the cauldron, where the goddess would examine the water within to see what form they would come back as a baby human or an animal with cubs.

The goddess's symbols included the crow, protection, prophecy, and strategy.

The Battle of Magh Tuired

Badb made a strong appearance in the first and second battles of Magh Turied. It was said that she appeared on the battlefield alongside her sisters in the form of a terrifying crow. She worked with her sisters to inspire terror in the hearts of their enemies, creating confusion with horrible prophecies they screamed together in the face of their foes. Her fierce cries echoed in the battle, foretelling the defeat of their rivals and the ominous end of the opposing army of Fomorians. These tactics were quite effective in driving the enemy back into the sea.

In another tale, it was said that after she left the battlefields, she would watch over families, becoming a faery (banshee) whose wail signaled the death of a family member.

The Prophetess

This is the story of the goddess who encountered King Cormac. The king, in need of a place to retire between battles, settles on a hostel owned by a man called Da Choca. As he rests with his soldiers, they notice an old woman washing bloodied clothes at the river. Intrigued, they questioned her, wanting to know what she was up to.

The crone then answers that she is washing the clothes of a king who will soon meet his demise. She appeared again to them in the hostel the same night, white-haired and dressed in red, instilling fear and a sense of horror in their hearts. On the same night, the king's enemies, the Connachta, invaded the hostel and murdered him, fulfilling the goddess's prophecy.

The Cailleach

Cailleach is associated with seasons and weather.
Internet Archive Book Images, No restrictions, via Wikimedia Commons:
https://commons.wikimedia.org/wiki/File:Wonder_tales_from_Scottish_myth_and_legend_(1917)
(14566397697).jpg

The Cailleach was associated more with seasons and weather rather than war and destruction. However, the season she was mostly connected to was winter, which in a lot of cultures is considered the withering season. She was known as the goddess of the cold and wind. She was said to be able to determine the length and harshness of winter.

The name of the goddess Caillech means the veiled one. Other opinions suggest that it is the root of other words that describe women, like "cailin," meaning girl.

Cailleach's influence is not limited to Ireland. Her presence was known in Scotland and the Isle of Man as well. She often appears as a veiled old hag with pale and blue skin. Her teeth were red, and she wore clothes decorated with skulls. She could leap across high mountains and ride storms.

Like most of the other deities, the Cailleach had the ability to shapeshift, taking on the form of a huge bird. The veiled goddess was also referred to as a creator deity. She was said to have been responsible for the shaping of the landscape. The tools she used for creation included a hammer she used to control thunder and storms (a close likeness to Thor of Asgard, the Norse God). In other tales, it said that she could control a well that would often overflow and flood the lands.

Stories often connected her with the cycle of life, fertility, death, and rebirth.

No one seemed to agree on whether or not this goddess was good or evil. It all depended on the tale and the narrator. She had a great love for wild and domesticated animals, specifically wolves (if you haven't noticed, there is a common theme regarding wolves among the Celts).

The Cailleach's presence is felt more in Irish and Scottish mythology, with little to no mention in Wales.

The Age of Cailleach

The story tells of a wandering friar and his scribe happening upon an old woman's house one day. The friar was curious about her age, to which she replied that she did not know exactly how long she'd been alive. However, she said she slaughtered an ox and made soup out of its bones every year. She told the friar that if he still wished to know her age, he was free to go into the attic and count the bones of the oxen left there.

The scribe climbed up the stairs and started throwing the bones to the friar so he could count. The friar kept note of the number of bones until he ran out of paper, and the pile of bones grew before him. The friar called to the scribe, who then told him that he hadn't even removed the pile from one corner of the attic, which indicated that Cailleach was a great age.

Cailleach's Influence on the Seasons

There was a seasonal division between Cailleach and Brigid. One ruled the winter and the other spring. In Scottish mythology, Cailleach transforms into Brigid with the coming of spring and then transforms back in winter.

Winter is heralded by the goddess, who rides a wolf and taps her magical staff on the Earth, turning it into ice.

Cailleach would go to the well of youth, drink, and change from a gloomy and chilly winter into a stunning young lady when she was through.

The change was the signal for the arrival of spring. This telling of the story encouraged many to believe that they were truly two parts of the same being, Brigid and the spring goddess, rather than two distinct entities.

In the tales that suggested that they were two different entities, Cailleach was believed to turn to stone at the end of winter, discarding her staff beneath a horse or a holly bush.

Because of the harsh nature of winter, the goddess was also linked to death. It was believed that she was responsible for gathering the souls of the departed. She would ride through the skies with the Wild Hunt during the winter solstice.

Chapter 9: Norse Goddesses

"Lo there do I see my Father; Lo there do I see my Mother, my sisters, and my brothers; Lo there do I see the line of my people, back to the beginning. Lo, they do call me, they bid me take my place among them, in the halls of Valhalla, where the brave may live forever."

Movie lovers would recognize this quote as the prayer recited by the Norse Vikings prior to the final battle in the historical masterpiece "The 13th Warrior". It didn't matter that the prayer was made up or historically unverified. The words summed up the lifestyle and beliefs by which the Norsemen led their lives. Their undying faith in their Gods. The high stature of warriors who die in battles and the spoils that await them on the other side.

In recent years, Norse mythology has gained a lot of traction due to the repeated and diverse portrayal of its stories in mainstream media. These stories presented the ancient characters as modern-day heroes.

Norse Goddess.
Internet Archive Book Images, No restrictions, via Wikimedia Commons.

Those who followed the pagan religion and remained immersed in the mythical tales following the emergence of Christianity were often referred to as heathens, a word derived from heaths, meaning the people who lived elsewhere in the countryside.

As you dive into the original stories that inspired these adaptations, you'll be faced with the conundrum of not being able to separate the light from the dark. It is a characteristic of the enthralling tales of the Nordic people that nothing was pure evil or pure good but a realistic mixture of both if you disregard the magic and powers.

Within this chapter, you'll find yourself swaying on the line between the peaks and valleys of morality as it explores the mighty goddesses of Asgard.

Hel

Hel is the patron of the dead and the underworld.
https://commons.wikimedia.org/wiki/File:Hel_(the_personification_of_Hel).png

She is the goddess whose namesake is the same as the place she ruled. Hel, also known as Hela, is the patron of the dead and the underworld. She also assumed the role of guardian of the souls who pass down Helvegr, the road of the dead.

The goddess's origins have been an open debate between scholars, with some believing that she was a demigod or a Jotunn rather than an actual deity. Most agree, however, that she is the daughter of the god Loki (the trickster) and the giantess Angrboda. She had two siblings, Fenrir, the wolf, and Jormungandr, the world serpent, both also the offspring of Loki.

Hel's outer appearance was unique. Scholars describe her as half-blue, like a giant, and half-flesh-colored, like a normal human. The duality of her appearance was thought to represent her two roles: as a patron of death and a guardian of the souls. In other tales, she is shown as a great beauty, with long flowing hair and a ghostly complexion. She was thought to be brutal, harsh, and menacing.

The Underworld

The name itself, "Hel," means *hidden* or *to cover* and is a term to describe the afterlife and the souls of the dead since they cannot be seen by the living. The kingdom was often referred to as "Niflheim," which roughly translates to the world of darkness.

Norse mythology places the dwelling of the dead right below one of the roots of the world tree, "Yggdrasill." In some stories, it is thought that Niflheim was the last of the nine realms where all the wrongdoers ended up. Others believed a guard dog named Garmr presided over the entrance of Hel, not unlike the Greek tales of the three-headed hound Cerberus. The Norse dog would howl at the arrival of new souls.

The kingdom where she ruled was said to lie downwards and northwards. The logic behind that is that people are buried below the ground, and the cold in the north resembles the frigid nature of the land of the dead. Niflheim or Hel was divided into separate sections, one of which was the shore of corpses," Nastrond." In Nastrond stood a huge castle swimming in serpent venom, where sinners such as murderers and adulterers suffered torment like none other. They were forced to endure the pain of having their blood sucked by the dragon Nidhogg when he wasn't snacking on the roots of Yggdrasil.

Other tales suggest that the land of Hel was not one of torment but rather a welcome reprieve for the frail and old, those who suffered the straw of death. Not all who died were sent to Niflheim. The drowned were claimed by the goddess Ran (the personification of the sea), the warriors were granted passage to Valhalla by Odin, and the common folk were taken to Folkvangr (field of the people), a land commanded by Freyja.

Mythology

When Loki's children arrived, a prophecy was declared to the Asgardian gods that the three younglings would cause distress and peril to the remaining deities. In an effort to counter the prediction, the All-Father Odin, king of the Gods, made his way to Jotunheim to bring the children back to Asgard, where he could keep a close eye on them.

To an outside eye, these actions resemble a paranoid yet concerned grandfather looking to change the fate of his grandchildren. That was far from the truth. While it is a fact that Odin was paranoid, his actions were not that of a loving grandparent. Immediately after collecting them, the king tossed the young serpent Jormungandr into the sea. He then threw Hela into the dark realm of Niflheim, tricking her into thinking that by doing so, she would be granted power over the nine realms of Norse cosmology. In truth, she was only allowed control over the dead souls that were passed down to her in the void that is Hel. For reasons unknown, Fenrir was kept with Odin in Asgard. Years passed, and the young wolf grew so strong and huge that the other gods feared they would be no match for the canine if he decided to turn against them. They came up with a plan to trick him into wearing manacles made by the dwarves, which were then used to hold him down on an island where he was stranded and left alone. At the same time, the little serpent was no longer little. He, too, had grown so large that he encircled the realm of Midgard (Earth), where the mortals lived, earning him the name the world serpent. In the meantime, Hela was reigning as queen of the underworld, no closer to escaping her fate than her subjects were.

Hel's Powers

Hels' abilities represent a paradox. Many view her as an evil spirit since she is a patron of death. However, in Norse mythology, she was considered a neutral, positive figure for taking on the role of caring for the souls of the deceased. Her powers were quite specific to the realm she commanded.

• Ruled Over the Underworld

Hela was in charge of allowing the souls into the land of the dead. She may have also been responsible for their judgment and the consequences assigned to them based on their deeds during their lives.

• Shapeshifter

Like her father, the goddess could change her appearance. Whether it is an eagle, a fox, or even a flurry of snow, she can probably take its form.

• Command Over Life and Death

The queen of the underworld had the ability to grant and take life, as she was the gatekeeper of the land of the dead. This power ensured that a balance was kept between the living and the dead.

Hel's Symbols

Every deity from ancient mythologies is linked to a series of symbols based on their traits and duties.

• A Spindle

This item is represented in different cultures as a metaphor for spinning the thread of life and death. It is associated with Hel based on the fact that she was granted the ability to take life or give it back, as well as keep the balance between the realms.

- **A Sickle**

The sickle symbolizes the end or the cutting off of the thread of life, which again is closely linked to Hel's powers over the dead.

- **A Hound**

Dogs represent loyalty, protection, and the ability to guard dwellings. All of these are qualities that Hel was thought to possess.

- **A Dragon or a Serpent**

Apart from being the sibling of the world serpent, when snakes shed their skin, it symbolizes rebirth, which could also mean rebirth in another realm.

Skadi

Skadi was a giantess.
https://commons.wikimedia.org/wiki/File:Skadi_Hunting_in_the_Mountains_by_H._L._M.jpg

Skadi is not considered a traditional goddess. Like Loki, she was a giantess who hailed from Jotunheim. In Norse mythology, most giants were described as unpleasant to behold, rough, and downright ugly. However, Skadi seemed to break that stereotype. Despite her blue complexion and huge physique, she was said to have had the features of a goddess. This fact was perpetuated by the truth that the gods appreciated beauty and would not have welcomed her into their fold otherwise.

The giantess was connected with cold and the hunt. She was known as a master skier, often portrayed with her ski shoes, quiver, and arrows. Unlike the rest of the giants, she had a calm nature and was not quick to anger or pick a fight. The lack of these usual giant characteristics did not take away from her strength and fierceness.

While a lot of tales portrayed the giants as evil spirits out to wage war against the gods, Skadi was one of the few believed to be free of any malicious intent despite her harsh and obstinate nature.

Skadi was a fresh addition to Norse mythology, often dominated by male figures. An independent, unwavering, self-reliant female who knows what she's owed, she was never afraid to fight for it.

Mythology

Skadi was the daughter of the giant Thiazi, who was known for his enmity with the Gods of Asgard. Guilty of stealing Idunn's apples (in other stories, he was guilty of forcing Loki to kidnap the goddess of youth, Idun), the giant was hunted down by the trickster Loki, who then fooled him into turning into an eagle and then killed him (in other tales, it is said that Thor was the one who took his life). Another version of the story suggests that as Loki was rescuing Idun at the behest of the gods, Thiazi transformed into an eagle and gave chase to the god of mischief. As they closed in on Asgard, the remaining gods created a firewall in the sky and killed the giant.

Though fully aware of her father's misdeed, Skadi was furious at the consequences that befell him at the hands of the Gods. After donning her armor, she made her way to Asgard to confront them and demand compensation for killing her father. In an effort to abstain from conflict, the gods of Azgard offered the young giantess a marriage proposal. Intrigued, Skadi agreed to the deal on the condition that they make an effort to make her laugh. The gods tried many jokes, but they all fell flat. In the end, Loki tied one end of a rope to a goat and the other end to his private parts. Loki would squeal in pain whenever the goat moved, making

Skadi laugh.

When it came to the marriage arrangement, despite her beauty, none of the gods were enthusiastic about marrying a giantess from Jotunheim. To settle the matter, she was allowed to choose her suitor from the lineup of gods only by looking at their feet. Secretly, the giantess was infatuated with Balder, the most handsome and kindest of all the gods. While examining the god's feet, she made an assumption that the most beautiful pair would for sure belong to Balder. She was sorely mistaken. When the veil was removed, she found herself face to face with the god Njord, patron of the sea and wind. Njord was much older than Balder and already had two other children, yet he had no wife.

Grudgingly, the pair honored the deal and sealed the marriage on the same day. The newlyweds were at a loss as to where to live. Njord loved the sea and shores, and Skadi enjoyed her time in the mountains and snow. Initially, they agreed to stay in each location for nine nights at a time, but that wasn't good enough for either of them, and they were both miserable with the arrangement. Eventually, they agreed to part ways amicably, forgoing their happily ever after. There is a mix of opinions regarding the fate of Skadi's love life following her failed marriage. Some say she lived alone in her icy castle, skiing to her heart's content on the slopes of the mountains. Others say that she married Ullr, the god of hunting and skiing, with whom she shared a lot of common interests. In several tales, it is believed that she even took Odin as a mate and had she bore several sons with him.

What most tales agree upon is that the giantess maintained her position as a goddess despite not being born as one. Despite her father's bad blood with the Asgardians and her short-lived marriage, she remained on good terms with the gods, even ready to lend a hand when they needed it.

It is said that she played a part in torturing the trickster for the role he played in killing Balder. She took part in tying him to a rock with a snake presiding over him and dripping venom on his face.

Skadi is known to have sided with the gods during Ragnarok against the other giants led by Loki. She was one of the survivors who got to see the dawn of the new world following the end of the gods.

Symbols

Skadi's name carries a lot of symbolism in and of itself. It is said that it is derived from the old Norse word "Skadi," meaning harm, which is a direct link to her being a giant, a race mostly associated with death, violence, and darkness, not to mention the start of her myth is all about avenging her father's death.

Another interpretation of the name suggests it comes from the Old High Germanic word "Scato," meaning shadow.

There is also an ongoing debate that her name is linked to Scandinavia, with some believing that she inspires the name of the land and others thinking that it's the other way around.

The goddess is also heavily associated with the mountains, snow, and hunting, not to mention her prowess in skiing. So naturally, her snow boots, bow, and arrow were symbols heavily influenced by her character.

It didn't matter whether people believed her to be a goddess or a giantess. Prayers and tributes were made in her favor so people wouldn't suffer harsh and unforgiving winters, specifically in the Norwegian mountains.

Angrboda

Angrboda was Loki's first wife.
https://commons.wikimedia.org/wiki/File:Lokis_Gez%C3%BCcht.jpg

Angrboda was yet another giantess from Jotunn and the first wife of the trickster Loki. She lived in a place called Ironwood (Jarnvid), which is a forest where the female Jotnar lived in Jotunheimr. Known as the mother of the monsters for giving birth to Loki's offspring Fenrir the wolf, Jormungandr the world serpent, and Hel, the guardian of the underworld.

Her name translates to "the one who brings grief," "she who offers sorrow," or "distress bringer." Names that foreshadow her dark influence in Norse mythology.

The goddess was often associated with chaos and destruction. Even though she is not mentioned as extensively as her counterparts in the Norse pantheon, that does not take away from the complexity and impact she had throughout the tales.

To be able to bear children such as Hel, Jormungandr, and Fenrir, you'd have to be a formidable character to start with. Her knowledge of magic and ability to recite prophecies was described in detail in the myths. Those gifts were often associated with the path of fate and destiny. It was also said that she could decipher the runes and see beyond the present into the future. Like many other deities, one of her notable talents included shapeshifting into various forms.

Mythology

The relationship between Angroboda and Loki was often a pain point when it came to her relationship with the rest of the gods. Even though they both loved each other deeply, and Loki had fathered all three of her children, in the eyes of the Asgardians, she was still a giantess. Loki's allegiance to the gods was always scrutinized due to his close relationship with his wife.

Considering her a threat, Odin ordered his son Thor to kidnap the giantess and bring her back to Asgard. The god of thunder complied and succeeded in capturing the mother of monsters. On her arrival, she was able to strike a deal with the gods: her freedom in exchange for giving up her children to the will of the gods. The Asgardians agreed to the exchange because they feared that her children were dangerous enough to bring upon them the end of the world, or the event known as Ragnarok.

Odin wasted no time in trapping Fenrir on an island, throwing Jormungandr in the sea, and imprisoning Hel in the underworld to rule over the dead. The gods were right to be nervous; Loki's children, especially Fenrir, played a huge part in bringing down the kingdom of Asgard. After breaking away from his chains on the Island, Fenrir howled at the doors of the underworld, releasing Hel's army of the undead. Fenrir is known to have fought a mighty battle with Odin prior to swallowing the all-father whole.

It is said that Angroboda participated in the battle against the gods in Ragnarok. Though her fate is uncertain, it is believed that she may have died during the march on the gods. Most scholars determined that she didn't get the chance to see the dawn of the new world that followed this cataclysmic event.

Symbols

Because her presence in Norse mythology and the stories that have been passed down through the generations is insufficient, her symbols are not common knowledge.

Angroboda was portrayed with hair the color of deep red blood, bluish skin, and a formidably muscular physique that resembled most giants of Jotunheim. She was an incarnation of misery and chaos, which is a common factor among the ice giants.

Chapter 10: Embracing the Dark Goddess Within

By guiding you as you form a connection with the divine feminine, this chapter takes you through the transformative journey of embracing the Dark Goddess within. It will give you plenty of practice, tips, and advice on how to acknowledge the shadow self and connect with the dark feminine energy within you.

Embracing the Dark Goddess within.
Internet Archive Book Images, No restrictions, via Wikimedia Commons.
https://commons.wikimedia.org/wiki/File:The_olive_fairy_book_(1907)_(14750441274).jpg

Your Inner Dark Goddess

The inner Dark Goddess can be viewed as part of your psyche and spirituality, making it a crucial tool for spiritual explorations. While most people think of darkness as something inherently flawed and destructive, embracing your inner divine feminine can teach you that this isn't the case. In fact, much of your personality and successes in all areas of life come from a balance between positive and negative forces within you. Still, many suppress their dark side due to societal expectations and widely accepted beliefs and traditions. You may be surprised that you're drawn to the divine feminine, but you aren't alone. Many people have experienced this over the centuries because they were drawn to it by their inner darkness – and for a good reason. The Dark Goddess within you can serve as an inspiration for your spiritual practices and a wonderful source of empowerment in times of need.

Do you wonder how you will know the goddess is awakening within you? Here are the telltale signs of the inner goddess at work:

- You experience self-doubt and insecurity, which results in envy and jealousy
- You have an immense fear of rejection and failure
- You are overly sensitive and prone to excessive emotional displays
- You strive for perfectionism and are driven by an intense need for control
- You overreact when someone disrespects your boundaries
- You tend to dwell on the past
- You find it easy to get people on your side or make them do whatever you want

While some of these may sound like negative traits, by going on this journey of self-discovery, you can learn why your goddess manifests the way she does and how to turn her manifestations in your favor. Self-discovery is having a better understanding of your desires, needs, feelings, and personality. Embracing the goddess through this process helps you improve your well-being and make better decisions, gives you a sense of purpose, enables you to build resilience and healthier relationships, gives you a chance to identify all your strengths and weaknesses, discover your passions and values, and much more.

Acknowledging the Shadow Self

You can work with your inner Dark Goddess in several ways. The psychological and spiritual approaches to working with and accepting the shadow self as a part of oneself vary and often depend on what goddess you identify with and what feels right for you in the present moment. Remember, the goddess, too, took different routes to embracing and showcasing dark and shadowy aspects.

Meditation and other mindfulness exercises, for example, are great ways to focus your attention on exploring the negative aspects of yourself (the manifestations of your shadow/inner Dark Goddess). On the other hand, positive affirmations can help acknowledge and accept the shadow traits, which may not be attractive but are all the more useful. All these practices can also serve as preparatory steps for forming a deeper connection with the inner goddess. They teach you how to tap into your intuition, which is central to spiritual communication (whether with your own inner spiritual self or a goddess).

Another recommendation is a practice called shadow work or shadow integration. Through this practice, you unpack the parts of your personality, thought patterns, complex emotions, and behavior you've been hiding. Unveiling the shadow hidden within the dark corners of your mind takes time, practice, and dedication. Through shadow integration, you explore why these parts of yourself are suppressed and how to find healthy ways to express them. Moreover, you'll transform these aspects of yourself into a controlled, disciplined expression of your darkness. Transferring the manifestation of your shadow from the unconscious to the conscious (so that it can assist you in navigating the world) is essential for embracing the Dark Goddess within and working with other dark feminine energies.

Shadow Visualization Technique

This visualization technique will introduce you to shadow integration and lay a foundation for further work with your shadow self.

Instructions:

1. Find a quiet place where you won't be disturbed - the exercise requires undivided attention.
2. Sit or lie down in a comfortable position and close your eyes.

3. Inhale through your mouth and exhale through your nostrils to relax.

4. As your mind struggles to settle, it will still wander for a few minutes (especially if you aren't used to deep relaxation/mindfulness exercises).

5. For the time being, allow your thoughts to run free without judgment.

6. Relax every part of your body. If you find it difficult to relax naturally, you can play some meditation music or sounds or burn incense in the background.

7. Once you relax, imagine yourself at a dark cave's entrance. Proceed to enter the cave.

8. As you walk through the entryway, you feel chilled air enveloping you.

9. You see a tiny light flickering in the distance and walk toward it. When you reach it, you see the light coming from a candle illuminating a shadowy figure standing behind it.

10. You instantly feel negativity coming out of the figure, yet you also feel drawn to it. Take note of where this ambiguity is mostly present in your body.

11. When you're ready, step closer to the shadow and ask them questions. Ask them who they are, if there is anything they want to tell or show you, or anything else you feel like asking.

12. You'll feel their answer deep within and realize the shadow is you. Take a mental note of who they say they are and what message they want to give you. This may be a negative feeling, memory, or thought you've been trying to repress for years.

13. Once you feel they've told you everything you needed to know or can handle at that time (it's okay if you can't handle embracing everything at once), let their image slowly fade away.

14. You can repeat this exercise many times. Each time you do, new insights will be revealed.

Connecting and Awakening Your Inner Dark Goddess

Here are even more recommended practices, rituals, and exercises to connect and awaken your inner Dark Goddess and explore their shadow self.

Working with Nature

The influence of the Dark Goddess can be felt everywhere in nature. Even walking barefoot in a small patch of grass will help you feel her magic. Take every chance you get to spend time in nature, even if it's for 10 minutes a day. If you live near a large body of water, and the weather allows it, go soak your feet and call on the goddess. Surround yourself with plants in your apartment if that's your only way of physically connecting with nature. Every bit helps you bond with the dark feminine.

Journaling

Whether you use it as a standalone practice or combined with another technique, journaling can be a powerful shadow exploration technique. You can jot down your experience with integration exercises. You can also use it to document your progress as you bond with your inner Dark Goddess. Write every day and read what you wrote at the end of the week. It'll allow you to recognize thoughts and emotions you weren't aware of. Even if you aren't sure of what to write or feel like you don't have anything to write, take out your journal and give your inner darkness free rein to express itself without censoring. You may notice you suddenly have a lot to write about!

Practicing Self-Cove

One of the best ways to embrace your shadow self is to practice self-love. By showing yourself some love, you're indicating that you're willing to embrace every part of yourself. Accepting yourself as you mean you're letting go of past burdens, making peace with your past mistakes and weaknesses, and giving your body, mind, and soul what they need the most.

Dark Moon Meditation

The following dark moon meditation will take you on a journey toward meeting your inner Dark Goddess and awakening her energy.

Instructions:

1. Find a quiet place where you can get comfortable and won't be disturbed. Settle your body and mind and take a few deep breaths.

2. Prepare your mind for a fictional journey into a forest - it can be a place you know but doesn't have to be. Following your instinct, find a clearing in the forest and light a fire.

3. After settling in front of the fire, set an intention to access the deepest parts of your soul. Take a deep breath and feel the air travel in your body - first upward to your crown, then down to your feet, and into the ground.

4. Now you've awakened both the dark energy within you and the Earth. Feel it travel up to your heart and outwards, enveloping you.

5. Feel the energy field extend around you toward the perimeter of the clearing, keeping you safe from everyone and everything around you.

6. Now, think about your plans for the following months. Feel the energy these goals evoke in you and channel them toward the fire before you. Think about what these plans mean to you, how they'll change your life, and who they'll make you become.

7. Let yourself drift into a deeper state of consciousness. Suddenly, you find yourself in the dark, enveloped only by the subtle light of the dark moon.

8. Allow yourself to adjust to the darkness. As you do, you feel more awakened, and your heart and mind open to new experiences.

9. Let go of all your fears, doubts, and thoughts you've created as a result of past trauma. Feel yourself being open to the unknown. Enjoy the freedom it brings you. You're now connected with the dark feminine.

10. Let the dark energy connect with your heart and soul, empowering you to speak your truth. Feel the goddess rise upward to your heart and even further into the universe.

11. When you're ready, take a deep breath and let the images and sensation go. Feel reassured in the knowledge that you're now unafraid of the unknown.

Chapter 11: Honoring the Dark Goddesses: Rituals and Practices

This final chapter offers practical guidance for those interested in actively engaging with the dark feminine deities. Ritual practices and patchwork can deepen your spiritual connection with the energy or the archetype of the Dark Goddesses. Besides teaching you how to do them, this chapter will also explain how to prepare for these practices.

Preparation and Setting

Having a sacred place as a center for your spiritual practice has numerous benefits for your connection with the Dark Goddess energy or archetype. By building an altar or similar area of worship, you're creating a space for invoking the goddess. Having a consistent space for your practices will also help you focus on your intention (a basic step you will need to take to manifest any desire, including your need to connect with the Dark Goddess). While creating a sacred space for practice, you'll also learn the goddess's correspondences - all the while expressing your creativity. By bringing together the right combination of elements, you can create a space for yourself, embracing all of your spirit, which will undoubtedly appeal to the Dark Goddess. You'll also get the chance to connect with nature.

Building an altar creates a space for invoking your inner goddess.
Rebecca Radcliff, CC BY-SA 2.0 <https://creativecommons.org/licenses/by-sa/2.0>, via Wikimedia Commons. https://commons.wikimedia.org/wiki/File:The_Imbolc_Ritual_Altar.jpg

From where you position it to the items you place on it, there are a lot of details that go into creating a sacred space. First and foremost, choose a fitting place, ideally in a quiet area in your home. If you don't have much space, you can always set up a small corner on your dresser, vanity table, inside your closet, or on the windowsill. You'll also need to keep in mind your physical and mental safety and well-being. Working with Dark Goddesses might involve lighting a candle or fire. Never leave these unattended. You should also prepare yourself for the emergence of negative thoughts and feelings. Make sure you're ready for this. If you're struggling with mental health issues or notice them while practicing, stop and only continue after consulting with a mental health professional.

Rituals for Connection

Meditating with a Symbol

One of the easiest ways to connect with a Dark Goddess is through one of her symbols. Meditating with her symbols will help you get into the right mind space to manifest your intention of connecting with the goddess. Draw a symbol of the goddess you want to summon on a piece of paper, meditate, and draw in her energy.

Instructions:

1. Start by assuming a comfortable position in a quiet room at night. Make sure you won't be disturbed for at least 10-15 minutes.

2. Take the symbol in your hands and greet the goddess:

   "Great Goddess, I greet you now

   The ruler of darkness and things unseen

   Caretaker of dark energies

   The divine feminine.

   I am ready to unite with you

   Please hear my summons and come to my side."

3. Visualize the symbol in front of your eyes.

4. Take a few breaths and focus on feeling the rich energy source stemming from the symbol.

5. Feel the goddess's power reaching you, enveloping your body. Feel it hyping you up to face your upcoming challenges.

6. Continue focusing on the symbol's energy until you feel prepared to complete your meditation.

7. When ready, let the image fade away.

8. Exhale deeply, and let your mind return to your everyday thoughts.

Journeying and Pathwork

Journeying and pathwork are both useful means to connect with Dark Goddesses on a deeper level. As they take you on a journey exploring thoughts and emotions, they foster self-reflection, especially if coupled with journaling.

The following meditation will help you meet and communicate with a Dark Goddess of your choice. You'll stay in one place for 8-10 minutes, so make sure to find a comfortable position and support for your back if needed.

Instructions:

1. Sit cross-legged on a mat. Rest your hand on your legs and make sure your back is relaxed without slouching.

2. Using your abdominal muscles, take three deep breaths. That way, your breathing becomes even deeper. Do it slowly with a long, audible sigh every time you exhale.

3. After the third exhale, examine your body to see if you're relaxed and comfortable or if you need to make any adjustments to your position.

4. Close your eyes and picture yourself walking along a dark, graveled path on a quiet night. Visualize a waning or new moon rising over the tree lines (the darker, the better).

5. Keep walking confidently forward in your vision, and try to revere in the solitude and companionship of the darkness around you. It's cold, and you can see the little puffs your breath makes in the chill of the late evening air.

6. As you walk, picture a flickering light up ahead of you. As you get closer, you'll see the light coming from far away. Walk toward it.

7. Next, visualize a small offering you're carrying in your hands. This could be anything you want to offer the goddess you're summoning.

8. Suddenly, the wind picks up, and you've reached your destination. A torchlit area surrounded by the vast darkness.

9. Take a deep breath and leave your offering while saying a quiet prayer to the goddess. As you do it, start focusing on your surroundings.

10. You suddenly pick up a source of energy in the air. If you feel unstable, visualize yourself grabbing something sturdy to keep yourself upright.

11. Now, picture the noise and the winds fading away and the night becoming silent and peaceful again. Your offering is now on the ground. However, as you turn slowly, you realize you're not alone.

12. You see the woman draped in a black cape approaching silently. After greeting her, feel free to look up at her face. See her eyes radiate with timeless wisdom.

13. Visualize her greeting and thanking you for visiting her in her sacred place. While she may look intimidating, you know you shouldn't be afraid of her because she is here to guide you through any difficulties you may face in the next stage of your life.

14. See the goddess turning away and slowly walking away from you. Take a deep breath, and let the journey take you back home. Take three slow, audible breaths to bring yourself back.

Sample Rituals and Meditations

Hekate Meditation at a Threshold

As a guardian of the crossroads, Hekate is the easiest to reach. Make sure the threshold you're using is undisturbed so you can focus on the exercise without interruption. Here is how to meditate with Hekate at a threshold:

1. Start at dusk, as it is another time of transition when the goddess's power to reach this world is at its strongest. Turn off all the lights and electronic devices nearby, and sit near the chosen threshold.

2. Lean your back against something supporting it, and place a cushion behind it. Take a deep breath and close your eyes.

3. Picture yourself walking uphill toward a small cottage. Stroll towards it, and don't fear entering it. Take a few deep breaths if you need to calm yourself.

4. See yourself entering a brightly lit cottage. As your eyes adjust to the lights, you'll see that the house is more spacious than it seemed from the outside. Suddenly, a female figure emerges and reaches what's revealed to be the crossroads.

5. See yourself smiling at Hekate as she smiles back at you and welcomes you with her nurturing energy. You can ask the goddess if there is anything she wants you to know as you start your journey together. If you aren't prepared to ask her anything, simply let her presence relax and empower you.

6. Let the image of Hekate disappear, but you can remain at the crossroads as long as you want to. You can even let yourself drift off to sleep if you wish.

7. When you're ready, leave the cottage. As you step outside, let yourself return to reality as you slowly open your eyes.

Night-Time Meditation with Nyx

This night-time meditation focuses on embracing the dark energy of Nyx, which is why it should be performed deep into the night. For practical purposes, it is recommended to choose a place near your altar where you can place a candle and light it for Nyx.

Instructions:

1. After lighting a candle for the goddess, turn off all the lights and sit in a comfortable position.

2. As you exhale, let go of any tension from your body and allow your mind to sink into a state of relaxedness and serenity.

3. Take another grounding breath and prepare to travel into the deep night.

4. You suddenly see yourself in a lush, green, earthy meadow at night. You start exploring the field as the sounds of the night accompany you.

5. Visualize an entrance in a tree near the meadow. As you cross the entryway, you start feeling the divine energy reaching out to you, making you more confident in your purpose.

6. Picture the goddess standing before you, dressed in a black robe. She offers her protection, and you accept it. Take in her picture and know that just as she survived many challenges, so will you until your soul's journey in this life is over.

7. Before you leave her side, offer the goddess a small token of gratitude as an offering. This could be a thought of worthlessness, prejudice, or any negative emotion you want to leave behind.

8. To fill the space left behind by the negative thoughts and emotions, the goddess offers you her blessings. Take three deep breaths as you accept and embrace them.

9. Let the emotions her energy evokes come to the surface. Whatever you feel - sadness, rage, anxiety, etc. - embrace them in the here and now.

10. After thanking her, walk back through the meadow, slowly bringing your awareness back to the present.

11. Once you're ready, open your eyes and feel revitalized and filled with positive energy.

Kali Invocation

The following Kali invocation will help you harness the goddess's energy when you feel the need for some internal purification. You'll need a representation of Kali.

Instructions:

1. Find a quiet space, light a candle for the goddess, and relax by breathing deeply for 5-10 minutes.

2. When you're ready, take three breaths to ground and center yourself. Then, visualize a bright light enveloping you.

3. Close your eyes and tell yourself you're safe and protected by the goddess.

4. Think about what upsets you, bringing every thought, emotion, and belief into your consciousness. Do this for five minutes or as long as it takes to become fully aware of everything that worries you.

5. Open your eyes and look at Kali's representation. Focusing on every detail of the image before you, tell yourself what you see. Do this for three minutes, and feel yourself saturated with Kali's essence.

6. Chant Kali's name for another three minutes, close your eyes, and focus on your intention of invoking the goddess.

7. As you feel her energy uniting with yours, take a few minutes to sit with her.

8. When you are ready, thank Kali for coming to your side and offering her empowered alignment.

9. Affirm you are safeguarded by her energy, and let your eyes open slowly.

Tables of Correspondences

Hecate

The goddess of witchcraft, night, necromancy, and the moon.

Equivalents

- The Roman goddess Trivia.
- The Irish Triple goddess the Morrigan.
- The Mesopotamian goddess Ereshkigal.
- The ancient Egyptian god Heka.

Colors

Main Colors:

- Black
- Red

White Other Colors:

- Blue
- Yellow

Offerings

- Round cakes
- Fish
- Honey
- Milk
- Mead and red wine

- Pomegranates
- Candles (preferably in the colors associated with her)
- Almonds
- Sage
- Yew
- Obsidian
- Quartz
- Seashells
- Feathers from owls, crows, or ravens
- Images, drawings, or sculptures of the moon

Symbols

- Keys
- Torches
- Hecate's Wheel

Moon Phases

The waxing crescent, full moon, and waning crescent symbolize her Triple Goddess archetype. The goddess is also celebrated on the dark moon.

Sacred Animals

- Dogs
- Crows
- Snakes
- Ravens
- Boars
- Horses

Sacred Numbers

- 3
- 7
- 13

Persephone

The goddess of Spring and fertility, and the Queen of the Underworld.

Equivalents

- The ancient Egyptian goddess Isis.
- The Norse goddess Hel.

Colors

Main Colors:

- Green
- Gold
- Red

Black Other Colors:

- Yellow
- Indigo
- Purple

Offerings

- Pomegranates
- A wreath of flowers.
- Roses, lilies, poppies, or other spring or wildflowers.
- Parsley
- Wheat
- Cypress
- Grains
- Honey
- Floral incense
- Boiled or smashed lemon balm, peppermint, or spearmint.
- Images or depictions of rams or bats.

Symbols

- Pomegranates
- Torches
- Grain seeds

Moon Phases

First Quarter

Sacred Animals

- Bats
- Rams
- Monkeys
- Parrots

Plants

- Pomegranate seeds
- Narcissus
- Lavender
- Willow tree
- Ivy
- Lily
- Daisy
- Maidenhair fern

Nyx

The primordial goddess of the night in ancient Greece.

Equivalents

- The Roman goddess Nox.
- The ancient Egyptian goddess Nephthys.

Colors

- Black
- Dark Green
- Indigo
- Violet

Offerings

- Red wine
- Dark feathers
- Black tea
- Coffee

- Roses, poppies, lilies, and any dark flowers.
- Incense
- Resin
- Molasses
- Dark berries
- Dark chocolate
- Celestial symbols

Symbols

- Black wings
- Dark clouds
- Egg
- Stars
- Black fog

Moon Phases

New moon

Sacred Animals

- Owls
- Dogs
- Bats

Sekhmet

The ancient Egyptian warrior goddess and the goddess of medicine.

Equivalents

- The Roman goddess Bellona.
- The Greek goddess Enyo.
- The Hindu goddess Kali.

Colors

- Red
- Orange
- Yellow

Offerings

- Red wine

- Incense
- Cat or lion depictions.
- Milk
- Fire
- Red gemstones like carnelian, garnet, and ruby.
- Spicy food

Symbols
- Red linen
- Lioness
- Sun disk

Herbs
- Catnip
- Basil
- Bay
- Patchouli
- Bloodroot

Nephthys

The ancient Egyptian protective goddess of the air.

Equivalents
- The Greek goddess Nyx.
- The Roman Goddess Nox.

Colors
- Black
- Red

Offerings
- Incense
- Black cloth
- Wine
- Water
- Bread
- Flowers

Symbols

- Vultures
- Sycamore trees

Sacred Animals

- Snakes
- Vultures
- crows

Plants

- Sycamore fig tree
- Papyrus
- Persea tree

Hathor

The ancient Egyptian goddess of the sky, women, love, and fertility.

Equivalents

- The Greek goddess Aphrodite
- The Roman goddess Venus

Colors

- Green
- Blue
- Black

Offerings

- Bread
- Wine
- Cheese
- Gemstones like malachite and turquoise.
- Copper and gold items.
- White, pink, or red candles.
- Jewelry
- Fabrics in her sacred colors.
- Mirrors

Symbols
- Cow
- Sun disk
- Sistrum
- Tree of Life

Herbs
- Rose
- Chamomile
- Myrrh
- Cinnamon
- Cider
- Jasmine

Nut

The ancient Egyptian goddess of the sky and the guardian of the vault of the heavens.

Equivalents
- The Greek god Uranus.

Colors
- Blue
- Black

Offerings
- Water
- Bread
- Fig
- Grapes
- Incense
- Candles
- Lanterns

Symbols
- Stars
- Water
- Pots

- Wind

Sacred Animals
- Bunnies
- Frogs
- Bees

Plants
- Lotus

Lilith

Mesopotamian figure of women's independence and freedom is associated with dark elements.

Equivalents
- Lamia from Greek mythology.

Colors
- Red
- Black

Offerings
- Candles in red, black, silver, and purple.
- Images or representations of the black moon.
- Owl and snake figurines.
- Paintings of the night sky and galaxy.
- Apples
- Red wine
- Apples
- Pomegranates

Symbols
- The triple moon
- The venus sign
- Wild rose

Moon Phases

Black moon

Sacred Animal
- Snake

Herbs

- Patchouli
- Wormwood
- Mandrake root
- Vervain
- Mugwort

Inanna

The Sumerian goddess of war, love, and fertility.

Equivalents

- The Greek goddess Aphrodite
- The Greek goddess Athena
- The Roman goddess Minerva
- The Roman goddess Venus
- The Canaanite goddess Astarte
- The Canaanite goddess Anate

Colors

- Green
- Black
- Red
- White
- Silver

Offerings

- Libations
- Grains
- Bread
- Dates
- Honey
- Incense
- Flowers like roses and lilies

Symbols

- Lion

- Eight-pointed star

Sacred Animals
- Lions
- Doves
- Bats
- Snakes
- Butterflies

Plants
- Lilies
- Reeds
- Myrtle
- Narcissus

Ereshkigal

The Sumerian horned goddess of the underworld.

Equivalents
- The Greek goddess Hecate

Colors
- Black
- Violet
- Dark brown

Offerings
- Bread
- Wine
- Beer
- Incense
- Pomegranate or lime juice
- Silver platters
- Plums
- Wheat
- Garlic
- Nutmeg

Symbols

- The cursing eye symbol
- The seven gates of the underworld
- Owls

Moon Phases

The dark and waning moon

Baba Yaga

Equivalents

- The Greek goddess Hecate
- The Celtic mythological figure Cailleach
- The Celtic goddess, The Morrigan

Colors

- Black
- Brown
- Dark Green

Offerings

- Bread
- Pancakes
- Crepe
- Butter
- Milk
- Cheese
- Vodka or wine

Symbols

- Mortar and pestle
- Oven
- Skull and bones

Moon Phases

The dark and waning moon

Sacred Animals

- Crow

• Raven

Marzanna/Morena

The Slavic goddess of death, rebirth, pestilence, and Winter.

Equivalents
- The Greek goddess Hecate
- The Greek goddess Demeter
- The Roman goddess Morta
- The Roman goddess Ceres

Colors
- Red
- White
- Black
- Green

Offerings
- Sickle
- Red and yellow apples
- Red beads
- Images of snakes and geese
- Stalks of grain
- A floral wreath
- Keys
- Honey
- Mead
- Beer
- Crystals

Symbols
- Birds
- Snakes
- Straw dolls

Sacred Animals
- Birds

- Snakes
- Frogs

Plants
- Grains
- Apple Trees
- Dyer's madder

Kali

The Hindu goddess of darkness, destruction, and death.

Equivalents
- The Egyptian goddess Sekhmet.
- The Celtic goddess, the Morrigan.

Colors
- Black
- Blue
- Red

Offerings
- Red millet
- Gemstones like red tourmaline, smoky quartz, and labradorite
- Red or white flowers
- Incense like jasmine and sandalwood
- Bananas
- Coconut

Symbols
- Sword
- Trident

Moon Phases

The dark and new moon

Sacred Animals
- Tiger
- Lion

Plants

- Hibiscus
- Narcissus

Durga

The Hindu goddess of war, destruction, and motherhood.

Equivalents

- The Greek goddess Athena
- The ancient Egyptian goddess Sekhmet

Colors

- White
- Red
- Blue
- Yellow
- Grey
- Orange
- Green

Offerings

- Sugar
- Traditional dishes like halwa and puri
- Red hibiscus flowers
- Jaggery
- Milk
- Coconut

Symbols

- Trident
- Conch shell

Moon Phases

The waxing moon

Sacred Animals

- Tiger
- Lion

Plants

- Rice plant
- Banana
- Arum plant
- Pomegranate
- Colocasia
- Sesbania sesban
- Wood apple
- Turmeric
- Ashoka tree

Chinnamasta

The Hindu goddess of divine feminine energy.

Colors

- Red
- Black

Offerings

- Flowers
- Incense
- Fruit
- Sweets

Symbols

- Sword

Chamunda

She is believed to be an aspect of the goddess Durga and is associated with transformation, protection, and destruction.

Equivalents

- The Hindu goddess Durga

Colors

- Red
- Black

Offerings

- Red or black flowers
- Incense, particularly jasmine or sandalwood
- Fruit
- Sweets

Symbols

- Trident

Elements

- Fire

Oya

The Santeria goddess of storms, lightning, and death.

Equivalents

- The Greek god Aeolus

Colors

- Brown
- Burgundy
- Purple

Offerings

- Plums
- Eggplant
- Red wine
- Meat
- Dark chocolate
- Crystals
- Cherries
- Grapes
- Plums
- Spicy food

Symbols

- Thunderbolt
- Niger River

- Wind
- Fire

Sacred Animals
- Vultures

Plants
- Croton plant

Sacred Numbers
- 9

Yewa

The Santeria goddess of death and virginity.

Colors
- White
- Pink
- Scarlet

Offerings
- Fish dishes
- Flowers
- Burgundy or black candles
- White wine
- Sweets

Symbols
- Bodies of water
- Pink veils
- Gravestones
- Cowry shells
- Mirrors

Moon Phases

Full moon

Sacred Animals
- Owl
- Fish

- Dolphins

Plants
- White lotus
- Lilies
- Chrysanthemums
- Orchid

Elements
- Water

Ala

The Igbo goddess of earth, morality, and fertility.

Equivalents
- The Roman goddess Ceres
- The Roman goddess Juno

Colors
- Red
- Brown

Offerings
- Kola nuts
- Yams
- Meat
- Palm wine
- Fruits

Symbols
- Yams

Moon Phases
- The crescent moon

Sacred Animals
- Python

Elements
- Earth

The Morrigan

The Irish goddess of war, witchcraft, and death.

Colors

- Red
- White
- Black
- Purple
- Indigo

Offerings

- Meat
- Apple
- Wine
- Feathers

Symbols

- Crows
- Ravens
- Feathers
- Candles
- Swords
- Axes
- Spears
- Shields
- The Moon

Moon Phases

The dark moon

Sacred Animals

- Wolves
- Cows
- Horses
- Scavenger birds

Plants and Herbs
- Belladonna
- Vervain
- Ginger
- Red clover
- Mugwort
- Thyme
- Blackthorn

Macha

The Celtic goddess of war.

Colors
- Red
- Green

Offerings
- Grain
- Milk
- Cheese
- Butter
- Apples
- Mead

Symbols
- Horses
- Crowns
- A sheaf of wheat

Sacred Animals and Plants
- Horses
- Grains
- Wheat

Elements
- Earth
- Water

Badb

The Celtic goddess of war and sovereignty.

Colors
- Black
- Red

Offerings
- Meat
- Fruits
- Wine

Symbols
- Crows
- Ravens
- Spears
- Cauldrons

Moon Phases

The dark and waning moon

Elements
- Earth
- Air
- Water

The Cailleach

The Celtic goddess of the cold and winds.

Colors
- Blue
- White
- Grey

Offerings
- Stones
- Whiskey
- Bread
- Oatcakes

- Items made of wool or fiber

Symbols
- Staffs
- Cauldrons
- Stones

Moon Phases
The dark and waning moon

Sacred Animals
- Hares
- Deer

Elements
- Earth

Hel

The Norse goddess of death and the underworld.

Colors
- Black
- Grey
- Dark blue

Offerings
- Coins and items of value
- White lilies
- Food and drink

Skadi

The giant wife of the god of the sea in Norse mythology.

Colors
- White
- Silver
- Blue

Offerings
- Meat
- Fish

- Stew
- Bread
- Crystals

Symbols
- Skis
- Snowflakes
- Hunting gear

Sacred Animals and Plants
- Wolves
- Evergreen trees

Angrboda

The bringer of grief in Norse mythology.

Colors
- Brown
- Green

Offerings
- Meat
- Mead
- Incense
- Stews
- Stones

Symbols
- Wolves
- Serpents
- Dragons
- Mountains

Elements
- Earth

Conclusion

The fascination with ancient cultures will never stop. History, mythology, religion, and culture have always intrigued the world. One of the most interesting parts of diverse cultures is their deities. Some people feel connected to either a god or a goddess. If the Dark Goddess is calling for you, your life will be transformed in more ways than one.

You started this book by learning about the concept and significance of the Dark Goddess and how it can be a powerful force of transformation. You also discovered its meaning, symbolism, and origins and how the archetypes and shadow self are associated with the Dark Goddess.

You then moved on to explore Dark Goddesses from every ancient culture. You started with the often misunderstood Greek goddesses Hecate, Persephone, and Nyx and their archetypal themes and characteristics.

Ancient Egypt is filled with mysteries. Learning about their deities will take you a step closer to uncovering their secrets. You discovered the mythology behind each Dark Goddess and their association with war, chaos, and death.

You then went on a journey to the world of two fascinating ancient cultures: the Mesopotamian and the Slavic. You explored the attributes, myths, and legends associated with them.

Ancient Hindu culture has been influential, but many people aren't familiar with their deities. You discovered the Dark Goddess's key characteristics, symbolism, and popular forms. You then traveled to ancient Africa and learned about their Orishas and the spiritual aspects behind them.

The Celtic and Norse cultures are very popular, and many people are familiar with their deities. However, less is known about their Dark Goddesses. You uncovered the mystery behind them as well as uncovering their mythology.

Finally, you learned about embracing the Dark Goddess within and connecting with the divine feminine. You discovered the psychological and spiritual approaches of the shadow self. You also learned rituals and practices to honor your Dark Goddess and deepen your connection with her energy.

Here's another book by Mari Silva that you might like

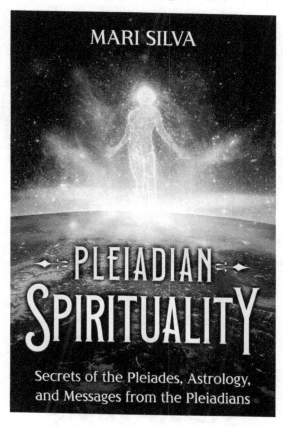

Your Free Gift
(only available for a limited time)

Thanks for getting this book! If you want to learn more about various spirituality topics, then join Mari Silva's community and get a free guided meditation MP3 for awakening your third eye. This guided meditation mp3 is designed to open and strengthen ones third eye so you can experience a higher state of consciousness. Simply visit the link below the image to get started.

https://spiritualityspot.com/meditation

Or, Scan the QR code!

References

(N.d.). Greekmythology.com. https://www.greekmythology.com/Other_Gods/Persephone/persephone.html

(N.d.). Greekmythology.com. https://www.greekmythology.com/Myths/Norse/Skadi/skadi.html

(N.d.). Owlcation.com. https://owlcation.com/humanities/TheCailleach

10 Benefits to Building Altars in Your Home. (n.d.). AuthorsDen.Com. https://www.authorsden.com/visit/viewarticle.asp?id=21959&AuthorID=32186

8 Phases Of The Moon — The Hoodwitch. (n.d.). The Hoodwitch. https://www.thehoodwitch.com/8-phases-of-the-moon

Abiola. (2016, May 14). Ala, Igbo goddess of Fertility and imagination! Today's African goddess affirmation card. Womanifest Your Power with Abiola: Spirit, Mindset, Success. https://womanifesting.com/ala-igbo-goddess-creativity/

Aesthetic, H. (2022, January 6). Goddess Chinnamastā or Pracaṇḍacaṇḍikā - hindu aesthetic - Medium. Medium. https://hinduaesthetic.medium.com/goddess-chinnamast%C4%81-c2786af73204

Africa, A. (2021, April 27). The Ancient Beliefs of African Goddesses. Amplify Africa. https://www.amplifyafrica.org/the-ancient-beliefs-of-african-goddesses/

Ala - Myth Encyclopedia - mythology, god, snake, life, people, African. (n.d.). Mythencyclopedia.com. http://www.mythencyclopedia.com/A-Am/Ala.html

Aletheia. (2015, April 4). What is shadow work? 7 exercises (+ free workbook). LonerWolf. https://lonerwolf.com/shadow-work-demons/

Amorim, K. (2019a, February 10). Durga - the warrior motherly goddess. -. Komala Amorim. https://www.komalaamorim.com/durga-the-warrior-motherly-goddess/

Amorim, K. (2019b, February 10). Kali - goddess of transformation, destruction, and transcendent energy –. Komala Amorim. https://www.komalaamorim.com/kali-goddess-of-transformation-destruction-and-transcendent-energy/

Andrews, A. M. (n.d.). The Divine Colors of Hathor. http://www.jewelry-history.com/2014/07/the-divine-colors-of-hathor.html

Angrboda (Giantess). (n.d.). Vikings Wiki; Fandom, Inc. https://vikings.fandom.com/wiki/Angrboda_(Giantess)

Bell, J. G. (2023, July 1). Nyx Goddess of the Night. The Hermetic Library Blog. https://library.hrmtc.com/2023/07/01/nyx-goddess-of-the-night/

Birch, L. (2022, March 3). Morana's Frozen Howl — A Deity for Angry Non-Binary Witches. Medium. https://lunarbirch.medium.com/moranas-frozen-howl-a-deity-for-angry-non-binary-witches-3dd05265b5a3

Cailleach – Mythopedia. (n.d.). Mythopedia. https://mythopedia.com/topics/cailleach

Cartwright, M. (2013). Kali. World History Encyclopedia. https://www.worldhistory.org/Kali/

Cartwright, M. (2021). The Mórrigan. World History Encyclopedia. https://www.worldhistory.org/The_Morrigan/

Chamunda Maa: The Hindu goddess of safety and protection. (2023a, February 22). Pujasthan. https://www.pujasthan.com/chamunda-maa-story-mantra-history/

Chiat, J. (n.d.). Russia Maslenitsa Festival - All You Can Eat Pancakes - Expat Explore. https://expatexplore.com/blog/maslenitsa-festival-russia-pancake-week/

Chinnamasta - the goddess who cut her head –. (2021, December 26). Hinduism Facts; Rahul. https://www.hinduismfacts.org/hindu-gods-and-goddesses/chinnamasta/

Complete chinnamasta mahavidya. (n.d.). Siddhaguru.org. https://www.siddhaguru.org/en/sri-chinnamasta-mahavidya

Cuba, A. pa mi. (2021a, April 26). What powers does the Orisha Yewá represent in the Yoruba Religion? Ashé pa mi Cuba. https://ashepamicuba.com/en/yewa-yoruba/

Cuba, A. pa mi. (2021b, September 1). Did you know these interesting qualities of Yewá? Goddess guess and pure. Ashé pa mi Cuba. https://ashepamicuba.com/en/orisha-yewa/

DanFF. (2022, March 17). Goddess Nyx - Greek Primordial Goddess of the Night. Santuário Lunar (Moon Shrine). https://www.santuariolunar.com/goddess-nyx/?expand_article=1

Dark Goddesses in Today's Society. (n.d.). The Veiled Crow. https://www.veiledcrow.com/service-page/dark-goddesses-in-today-s-society

Das, S. (2007, June 15). 10 of the most important Hindu gods. Learn Religions. https://www.learnreligions.com/top-hindu-deities-1770309

Das, S. (2008, April 16). Kali: The Dark Mother goddess in Hinduism. Learn Religions. https://www.learnreligions.com/kali-the-dark-mother-1770364

Davidson, L. (n.d.). Sekhmet: The ancient Egyptian goddess of war. History Hit. https://www.historyhit.com/sekhmet-the-ancient-egyptian-goddess-of-war/

Deleted. (n.d.). Hecate in different mythologies : r/mythology. https://www.reddit.com/r/mythology/comments/nipys7/hecate_in_different_myth ologies/

DK Find Out! (n.d.). DK Find Out! https://www.dkfindout.com/us/history/ancient-egypt/sekhmet/

Domitrovich, M. (2015, September 27). The invocation of Kali. EDIBLESPIRIT. https://ediblespirit.com/eatyourspirit/2015/9/27/trim-your-dingleberries-or-the-invocation-of-kali

Dunlop, S. (n.d.-a). Macha. Bardmythologies.com. https://bardmythologies.com/macha/

Dunlop, S. (n.d.-b). The curse of Macha. Bardmythologies.com. https://bardmythologies.com/the-curse-of-macha/

Ebede, F. (2023, March 3). Dark Feminine Energy: How To Embrace It And Unleash Your Inner Goddess. Selfhealjourney.Com. https://selfhealjourney.com/2023/03/03/dark-feminine-energy/

Eclectic Witchcraft. (2023, October 13). Ways To Represent Lilith On Your Pagan Altar - Eclectic Witchcraft. https://eclecticwitchcraft.com/ways-to-represent-lilith-on-your-pagan-altar/

Ereškigal (goddess). (n.d.). http://oracc.museum.upenn.edu/amgg/listofdeities/erekigal/index.html

Establishing the temple of Nephthys. (2021, December 19). Isiopolis. https://isiopolis.com/2021/12/19/establishing-the-temple-of-nephthys/

Eze, C. (2023, March 19). Oya, the Yoruba rain goddess. The Guardian Nigeria News - Nigeria and World News; Guardian Nigeria. https://guardian.ng/life/oya-the-yoruba-rain-goddess/

Fields, K. (2018, December 20). Dark Goddesses: Our 15 FAVORITES From Around the World. Otherworldly Oracle. https://otherworldlyoracle.com/dark-goddesses-list-descriptions/

Fields, K. (2019, November 25). Hathor Goddess of Love: How to work with her for Love & passion. Otherworldly Oracle; FIELDS CREATIVE CONSULTING. https://otherworldlyoracle.com/egyptian-goddess-of-love/

Goddess Ala. (2012, March 14). Journeying to the Goddess. https://journeyingtothegoddess.wordpress.com/2012/03/14/goddess-ala/

Goddess Baba Yaga. (2013, June 7). Journeying to the Goddess. https://journeyingtothegoddess.wordpress.com/2012/08/31/goddess-baba-yaga/

Goddess Hathor: Three ways of mentoring the dead. -. (2020, May 18). María Rosa Valdesogo. https://www.mariarosavaldesogo.com/goddess-hathor-three-ways-mentoring-the-dead/

Goddess Hecate Moon Phase Necklace, Triple Goddess Symbol — Bang-Up Betty. (n.d.). Bang-Up Betty. https://www.bangupbetty.com/siren/hecate-moon-phase-necklace

Goddess Kali. (2013, June 7). Journeying to the Goddess. https://journeyingtothegoddess.wordpress.com/2012/02/24/goddess-kali/

Hair, Hathor and moon. (2013, July 7). HAIR AND DEATH IN ANCIENT EGYPT. https://hairanddeathinancientegypt.com/2013/07/08/hathor-moon-and-hair/

Hannah. (2022, February 14). Comparing Egyptian, Roman, and Greek gods - Hannah Fielding. Hannah Fielding. https://hannahfielding.net/egyptian-roman-greek-gods/

Hardy, J. (2023, April 24). Chaos and Destruction: The symbolism of Angrboda in Norse Mythology and Beyond | History Cooperative. History Cooperative. https://historycooperative.org/angrboda/

Hardy, J. (2023a, March 10). Skadi: The Norse goddess of skiing, hunting, and pranks. History Cooperative; The History Cooperative. https://historycooperative.org/skadi/

Hathor. (n.d.). Mythopedia. https://mythopedia.com/topics/hathor

Heal the Soul through Meditation. (2019, April 21). Science of Spirituality. https://www.sos.org/heal-the-soul-through-meditation/

Hel (The Underworld). (2012, November 15). Norse Mythology for Smart People. https://norse-mythology.org/cosmology/the-nine-worlds/helheim/

Hel. (n.d.). Mythos and Legends Wiki; Fandom, Inc. https://mythos-and-legends.fandom.com/wiki/Hel

Herukhuti, R. A. (2023, October 14). Nut: The Black Mother Goddess of Egypt. Afrikaiswoke.com. https://www.afrikaiswoke.com/nut-the-black-mother-goddess-of-egypt/

Hirst, K. K. (2019, October 28). Marzanna, Slavic Goddess of Death and Winter. ThoughtCo. https://www.thoughtco.com/marzanna-4774267

Hoseck, N. (2023, January 31). The Morrigan: A goddess of fate, war, and death. Ireland Wide. https://www.irelandwide.com/the-morrigan/

How to embrace & integrate your shadow self for major healing. (2021, November 11). Mindbodygreen. https://www.mindbodygreen.com/articles/shadow-self

Huanaco, F. (2022, February 11). Persephone: Goddess Correspondences, Symbols & Myth. Spells8. https://spells8.com/lessons/persephone-goddess/

Inana/Ištar (goddess). (n.d.). http://oracc.museum.upenn.edu/amgg/listofdeities/inanaitar/

Insight Network, Inc. (n.d.). Awaken The Dark Moon Goddess Within. Insighttimer.Com. https://insighttimer.com/soulvisionary/guided-meditations/awaken-the-dark-moon-goddess-within

Iwalaiye, T. (2023, March 3). African deities: Who is goddess Oya? Pulse Nigeria. https://www.pulse.ng/lifestyle/food-travel/african-deities-who-is-goddess-oya/q5gf7h2

Jay, S. (2022, July 18). How To Embrace Dark Feminine Energy & Unleash Your Power. Revoloon. https://revoloon.com/shanijay/dark-feminine-energy

Jessica, S. (2019, July 28). Angrboda Norse mythology. Norse and Viking Mythology; vkngjewelry. https://blog.vkngjewelry.com/en/angrboda/

Joe, J. (2022a, January 11). Nephthys: The ancient Egyptian goddess of air and betrayal. Timeless Myths. https://www.timelessmyths.com/mythology/nephthys/

Joe, J. (2022b, March 8). Sekhmet: The warrior goddess and protector of the Egyptian pharaohs. Timeless Myths. https://www.timelessmyths.com/mythology/sekhmet/

JSouthernStudio. (n.d.). Hecate: Deities & Demons. JSouthernStudio. https://www.jsouthernstudio.com/blogs/esotericinsights/hecate-goddess-of-the-month-october-2019

Kabir, S. R. (2023, January 12). Hel: Norse goddess of death and the underworld. History Cooperative; The History Cooperative. https://historycooperative.org/hel-norse-goddess-of-death/

Kabir, S. R. (2023, March 20). The Morrigan: Celtic goddess of war and fate. History Cooperative; The History Cooperative. https://historycooperative.org/morrigan/

Keys, K. H. (n.d.-a). Hekate and the Moon: History and Rituals. Keeping Her Keys. https://keepingherkeys.com/blog/f/hekate-and-the-moon-history-and-rituals

Keys, K. H. (n.d.-b). Hekate's Colors, Numbers, Stones And Symbols. Keeping Her Keys. https://keepingherkeys.com/f/hekates-colors-numbers-stones-and-symbols

Khamesra, M. (2021, October 23). Goddess Chamunda Devi (Matrika). Manish Jaishree; Jaishree Khamesra. https://manishjaishree.com/chamunda/

Kolton, M. (2023, August 23). Working with the Dark Goddess: A Journey Through the Dark Night of the Soul. Medium. https://alchemicalwombgoddess.medium.com/working-with-the-dark-goddess-a-journey-through-the-dark-night-of-the-soul-8bcbfe3d506e

Kyteler, E. (2023, August 4). Hekate's Sacred Animals: Symbolic Meanings of Dogs, Crows, and Snakes - Eclectic Witchcraft. Eclectic Witchcraft. https://eclecticwitchcraft.com/hekates-sacred-animals/

Landious Travel. (2022, April 9). Goddess Sekhmet - Iconography and Symbolism - Landious Travel. https://landioustravel.com/egypt/egyptian-deities/goddess-sekhmet/

Lee, K. A. (2022, April 6). 13 Formidable Examples of the Dark Goddess for 2023. The Moon School. https://www.themoonschool.org/divine-feminine/moon-goddess-series/what-is-the-dark-goddess-plus-13/

Lilith Archetype - 10 benefits of the "dark feminine" model. (2022, September 24). Santuário Lunar (Moon Shrine). https://www.santuariolunar.com/lilith-archetype/

Lilith. (n.d.). Fmarion.Edu. https://people.fmarion.edu/llarsen/LilithExplained.htm

Lockett, R. (2023, March 1). Cailleach: The Celtic goddess of winter. History Cooperative; The History Cooperative. https://historycooperative.org/cailleach/

López, J. S. (2021, October 26). Yewa - Yoruba Goddess of virginity and death. Symbol Sage. https://symbolsage.com/yewa-goddess-of-death/

Luna, B. (2016, August 22). Deep healing with A dark mother: Working with tantric goddess Chamunda —. The Hoodwitch. https://www.thehoodwitch.com/blog/2016/8/22/deep-healing-with-a-dark-mother-chamunda

Macha mythology project ms.Mc Cormac 6th class. (2022, November 23). Ennis National School. https://www.ennisns.ie/class-life-post/macha-mythology-project-ms-mc-cormack-6th-class/

Macha. (n.d.). Brooklynmuseum.org. https://www.brooklynmuseum.org/eascfa/dinner_party/heritage_floor/macha

Mackay, D. (2021, June 27). Everything you need to know about Hecate (maiden, mother, crone). TheCollector. https://www.thecollector.com/hecate-goddess-magic-witchcraft/

Mark, J. J. (2009). Hathor. World History Encyclopedia. https://www.worldhistory.org/Hathor/

Mark, J. J. (2010). Inanna. World History Encyclopedia. https://www.worldhistory.org/Inanna/

Mark, J. J. (2016). Nephthys. World History Encyclopedia. https://www.worldhistory.org/Nephthys/

Mark, J. J. (2017a). Ereshkigal. World History Encyclopedia. https://www.worldhistory.org/Ereshkigal/

Mark, J. J. (2019). Field of Reeds (aaru). World History Encyclopedia. https://www.worldhistory.org/Field_of_Reeds/

Mark, J. J. (2021). Hel. World History Encyclopedia. https://www.worldhistory.org/Hel/

Mark, J. J. (2021). Orisha. World History Encyclopedia. https://www.worldhistory.org/Orisha/

Mark, J. J. (2022). Inanna. World History Encyclopedia. https://www.worldhistory.org/Inanna/

Mark, J. J. (2023). Baba Yaga. World History Encyclopedia. https://www.worldhistory.org/Baba_Yaga/

Medium. (n.d.). Medium. https://medium.com/@judithshaw20/the-dark-goddess-empowers-consciousness-shifts-part-2-10fef83b0ba8

Meet the Dark Goddesses. (n.d.). The College of Psychic Studies. https://www.collegeofpsychicstudies.co.uk/enlighten/meet-the-dark-goddesses/

Meeting Hekate at Her Crossroads - Guided Meditation. (n.d.). SoundCloud. https://soundcloud.com/thewitchespath/meeting-hekate-at-her-crossroads-guided-meditation

Miate, L. (2022). Nyx. World History Encyclopedia. https://www.worldhistory.org/Nyx/

Mooney, S. (2020, June 20). The goddess Macha. Tales From The Wood. https://talesfromthewood.ie/the-goddess-macha-warrior-mother-and-queen/

Morana (Marzanna, Marena). (n.d.). Aminoapps. https://aminoapps.com/c/pagans-witches/page/item/morana-marzanna-marena/MQdW_bnET0I2kjkb1Lwm1mQN7nnZYPw3e4e

Morrigan, J. (2018, June 20). Litha Ritual for Nephthys. Pagan Muses. https://paganmuses.com/2018/06/21/litha-nephthys/

Morrigan. (n.d.). Mythopedia. https://mythopedia.com/topics/morrigan

Mythology, C. T. C. (2019, September 22). Sekhmet. Constructed Mythology. https://conmyth.fandom.com/wiki/Sekhmet

Nair, N. (2023, July 16). Unveiling the dark side: Evil Greek goddesses in mythology. Mythlok. https://mythlok.com/evil-greek-goddesses/

Nephthys | Egyptian Goddess of Death, Mythology & Symbolism | Study.com. (n.d.). study.com. https://study.com/academy/lesson/nephthys-facts-mythology-egyptian-goddess-death.html

Nephthys. (n.d.). https://occult-world.com/nephthys/

Nephthys. (n.d.). Mythopedia. https://mythopedia.com/topics/nephthys

New York Latin Culture Magazine. (2023, August 11). Yewá dances in the cemetery to help the dead move on. New York Latin Culture Magazine®. https://www.newyorklatinculture.com/yewa-dances-in-the-cemetery-to-help-the-dead-move-on/

Noble, B. (2021, June 18). Marzanna/Morana - Slavic Goddess of Winter, Pestilence, and Death - Slavic Mythology Saturday - Brendan Noble. Brendan Noble. https://brendan-noble.com/marzanna-morana-goddess-of-winter-pestilence-and-death/

NORSE GODS: HEL – Ýdalir. (n.d.). Ydalir.Ca. https://ydalir.ca/norsegods/hel/

Norse mythology for Smart People - the ultimate online guide to Norse mythology and religion. (2012, November 14). Norse Mythology for Smart People. https://norse-mythology.org/

Nut - explore deities of ancient Egypt. (n.d.). Egyptianmuseum.org. https://egyptianmuseum.org/deities-nut

Nut –. (n.d.). Mythopedia. https://mythopedia.com/topics/nut

Nyx – Mythopedia. (n.d.). Mythopedia. https://mythopedia.com/topics/nyx

O'Connor, D. (2023, May 15). Cailleach - Irish goddess of the winter & her trail in Ireland. Irishcentral.com. https://www.irishcentral.com/travel/best-of-ireland/cailleach-irish-goddess-winter-trail-ireland

O'Hara, K. (2023, June 29). The Morrigan: The story of the fiercest goddess in Irish myth. The Irish Road Trip. https://www.theirishroadtrip.com/the-morrigan/

Oakes, H. (2019, April 9). Chinnamasta: The archetypal figure of the unconscious — Hayley Oakes, LM CPM. Hayley Oakes, LM CPM. https://www.hayleyoakes.com/articles/chinnamasta-the-archetypal-figure-of-the-unconscious

Ojukutu-Macauley, L. (2021, March 8). Women's International Day – West African earth goddess. Imọlẹ Candles. https://imolecandles.co.uk/blogs/news-1/women-s-international-day-west-african-earth-goddess

OldWorldGods. (2023, October 20). Celtic goddess Badb: Unveiling the mysterious power of the Battle Crow. Old World Gods. https://oldworldgods.com/celtics/celtic-goddess-badb/

Oliver, C. (2022, April 7). Angrboda. Vikings of Valhalla US. https://vikings-valhalla.com/blogs/norse-mythology/angrboda-norse-mythology

Onlinepuja. (n.d.). Steps to worship Goddess Durga. Onlinepuja.com. https://www.onlinepuja.com/blog/steps-worship-goddess-durga

Original Products. (2023, March 1). Orisha Oya: Ruler of storms and the wind. Original Botanica; www.originalbotanica.com#creator. https://originalbotanica.com/blog/orishas-oya-santeria

Oya, great goddess of the Wind. (n.d.). African American Wiccan Society. https://www.aawiccan.org/oya

Parikh, A. (2023, March 13). Sekhmet: Egypt's forgotten esoteric goddess. History Cooperative; The History Cooperative. https://historycooperative.org/sekhmet/

Pascale, S. (2020, September 16). The divine feminine. The Light Collective | Yoga Studio & Training - by Sian Pascale. https://www.thelightcollective.yoga/journal/durgamaa

Pchr, R. (2023, July 23). Chamunda: Unraveling the divine enigma. Braj Vrindavan Yatra. https://brajvrindavanyatra.com/2023/07/23/chamunda-unraveling-the-divine-enigma/

PERSEPHONE. (n.d.). Theoi.com. https://www.theoi.com/Khthonios/Persephone.html

Porteus, S. (2021, April 9). Baba Yaga — Creative Countryside. Creative Countryside. https://www.creativecountryside.com/blog/baba-yaga

Rajhans, S. G. (2007, October 15). The goddess Durga: The mother of the Hindu universe. Learn Religions. https://www.learnreligions.com/goddess-durga-1770363

Ramesh. (2019, September 1). Chinnamasta - the headless tantric goddess of transformation. VedicFeed. https://vedicfeed.com/chinnamasta-goddess-of-transformation/

Rhys, D. (2020, November 27). Badb - the Celtic goddess of war. Symbol Sage. https://symbolsage.com/badb-celtic-war-goddess/

Rhys, D. (2020, October 20). Skadi – Norse goddess of mountains and hunting. Symbol Sage. https://symbolsage.com/skadi-norse-goddess-hunting/

Rhys, D. (2021, January 7). Goddess Kali: The Hindu mother, warrior, and protector. Symbol Sage. https://symbolsage.com/kali-goddess-of-hinduism/

Rhys, D. (2022, April 18). Oya – the African goddess of weather. Symbol Sage. https://symbolsage.com/oya-goddess-of-weather/

Rhys, D. (2023, April 26). Nephthys - goddess of darkness and death in Egyptian mythology. Symbol Sage. https://symbolsage.com/nephthys-goddess-of-darkness-egyptian/

Rhys, D. (2023, February 7). The deep symbolism and powers of goddess Durga (Hinduism). Symbol Sage. https://symbolsage.com/durga-goddess-of-hinduism/

Richard. (2023, January 1). Who is Angrboda in Norse Mythology? The Giantess Grief-Bringer. Mythologyplanet.com. https://mythologyplanet.com/angrboda-norse-mythology-grief-bringer/

Rokvity, A. (2019, September 30). Goddess Durga: The embodiment of pure force. Yogapedia.com; Goddess Durga: The Embodiment of Pure Force. https://www.yogapedia.com/goddess-durga-the-embodiment-of-pure-force/2/11758

Scarletarosa. (2019, September 6). Ereshkigal. Tumblr. https://scarletarosa.tumblr.com/post/187530004051/ereshkigalmesopotamian-goddess-of-death-queen-of

Sekhmet. (n.d.). Egyptianmuseum.org. https://egyptianmuseum.org/deities-sekhmet

Sever, A. (2023, February 17). Hathor, the Goddess of Love: Powers, Rituals, Prayers, Offerings. Occultist. https://occultist.net/goddess-hathor-ritual-prayers-powers/

Shabnamdeep. (2023, September 13). The origins and myths of Goddess Durga. Goddess Gift. https://goddessgift.com/goddesses/durga/

SHADES OF A GODDESS - By Johnny Guthrie - Google Arts & Culture. (n.d.). Google Arts & Culture. https://artsandculture.google.com/usergallery/SgIS2pLQrfZaIQ

Sharma, M. (2023, October 17). Navratri 2023: How to worship Goddess Durga during Navaratri festival. Times Of India. https://timesofindia.indiatimes.com/religion/festivals/navratri-2023-how-to-worship-goddess-durga-during-navaratri-festival/articleshow/104494008.cms

Shaw, J. (2023, July 26). The Dark Goddess Empowers Consciousness Shifts, Part 1. Medium. https://medium.com/@judithshaw20/the-dark-goddess-empowers-consciousness-shifts-part-1-20ac63df5a63

Sir, P. (2021, October 24). Skadi Norse goddess facts and symbols meaning. Pirate Jewelry. https://piratejewellery.com/norse-mythology/skadi-norse-goddess-facts-and-symbols-meaning/

Skadi – the giantess who married the sea god. (n.d.). Historiska.Se. https://historiska.se/norse-mythology/skadi-en/

Skadi (mythology). (n.d.). Heroes Wiki; Fandom, Inc. https://hero.fandom.com/wiki/Skadi_(mythology)

Skadi goddess of winter. (2021, March 26). The Danish Canadian. https://www.danishcanadianmuseum.com/post/skadi-goddess-of-winter

Skadi. (2012, November 15). Norse Mythology for Smart People. https://norse-mythology.org/gods-and-creatures/giants/skadi/

Skadi. (n.d.). Newworldencyclopedia.org. https://www.newworldencyclopedia.org/entry/Skadi

Skjalden. (2020a, August 11). Angrboda. Nordic Culture. https://skjalden.com/angrboda/

Skjalden. (2020b, August 27). Hel is NOT the Norse Goddess of Death - Norse Mythology. Nordic Culture. https://skjalden.com/hel/

Slavs, M. T., & Slavs, M. T. (2022, May 14). Marzanna or Morana: Slavic Goddess of Death. Meet the Slavs. https://meettheslavs.com/marzanna-or-morana/

Smith, M. (2023, September 10). Badb. Goddess Gift; The Goddess Path. https://goddessgift.com/goddesses/badb/

Stanic, Z. (2023, April 7). Oya – Santeria goddess of storm, lightning, and death. Goddess Gift; The Goddess Path. https://goddessgift.com/goddesses/oya/

Stanic, Z. (2023b, September 12). The Morrigan – Celtic goddess of death, war and transformation. Goddess Gift. https://goddessgift.com/goddesses/the-morrigan/

Stanic, Z. (2023c, September 12). Yewa – Santeria Goddess of death and virginity. Goddess Gift. https://goddessgift.com/goddesses/yewa/

Sullivan, K. (2016, November 26). The mythology of nut, mother of gods. Ancient Origins. https://www.ancient-origins.net/myths-legends/mythology-nut-mother-gods-007084

tea and rosemary. (2021, April 21). 8+ Incredible Dark Goddesses & How To Work With Them. Tea & Rosemary. https://teaandrosemary.com/dark-goddesses/

Terravara. (2022, December 22). Working with Sekhmet: Offerings, Herbs, Crystals & More. Terravara. https://www.terravara.com/working-with-sekhmet/

The Dark Goddess As Archetype. (2010, November 1). Rounwytha. https://rounwytha.wordpress.com/2010/11/01/the-dark-goddess-as-archetype/

The Dark Goddess: A Post-Jungian Interpretation. (2018, October 19). The Religious Studies Project. https://www.religiousstudiesproject.com/response/the-dark-goddess-a-post-jungian-interpretation/

The Editors of Encyclopaedia Britannica. (1998, July 20). Baba Yaga | Characteristics, Family, & Mischief. Encyclopedia Britannica. https://www.britannica.com/topic/Baba-Yaga

The Editors of Encyclopaedia Britannica. (1998, July 20). Ereshkigal | Underworld, Queen, Sumerian. Encyclopedia Britannica. https://www.britannica.com/topic/Ereshkigal

The Editors of Encyclopaedia Britannica. (2023a, September 8). Hathor | Mother Goddess, Sky Goddess, Cow Goddess. Encyclopedia Britannica. https://www.britannica.com/topic/Hathor-Egyptian-goddess

The Editors of Encyclopaedia Britannica. (2023b, September 25). Skadi | Goddess, Jotun, Hunting. Encyclopedia Britannica. https://www.britannica.com/topic/Skadi

The Editors of Encyclopaedia Britannica. (2023c, October 23). Nut | Sky, Moon & Stars. Encyclopedia Britannica. https://www.britannica.com/topic/Nut-Egyptian-goddess

The Editors of Encyclopedia Britannica. (2022). Ishtar. In Encyclopedia Britannica.

The Editors of Encyclopedia Britannica. (2022). Niflheim. In Encyclopedia Britannica.

The Editors of Encyclopedia Britannica. (2023). Skadi. In Encyclopedia Britannica.

The Sect of the Horned God. (2023, February 25). The Dark Goddess Archetype. The Sect of the Horned God. https://www.thesectofthehornedgod.com/?p=5624

Thebacchichuntress. (2015, August 20). Offerings to Nyx. Tumblr. https://thebacchichuntress.tumblr.com/post/127160005123/offerings-to-nyx

Tlredmond. (2017, December 6). Characteristics – Baba Yaga. https://diorite.roanoke.edu/students/Fall2017/INQ270G3/tlredmond/?p=94

Tolentino, C. (2023, February 3). Macha: War Goddess of Ancient Ireland | History Cooperative. History Cooperative. https://historycooperative.org/macha/

Tolentino, C. (2023, January 30). Macha: War goddess of ancient Ireland. History Cooperative; The History Cooperative. https://historycooperative.org/macha/

Took, T. (n.d.). Lilith, Sumerian Demon Goddess and First Wife of Adam. Thaliatook.Com. https://www.thaliatook.com/AMGG/lilith.php

Turnbull, L. (2023, April 7). Nut - Egyptian "mother of all gods." Goddess Gift; The Goddess Path. https://goddessgift.com/goddesses/nut/

Turnbull, L. (2023a, September 12). Inanna: Ancient Sumerian Goddess of Heaven. Goddess Gift. https://goddessgift.com/goddesses/inanna/

Turnbull, L. (2023b, September 12). Nut: Egyptian Goddess 'Mother of All Gods.' Goddess Gift. https://goddessgift.com/goddesses/nut/

Turnbull, L. (2023c, September 12). Persephone: Greek Goddess Of Innocence And Queen Of The Underworld. Goddess Gift. https://goddessgift.com/goddesses/persephone/

Twelfthremedy. (2020, April 11). Hecate offerings. Tumblr. https://twelfthremedy.tumblr.com/post/615056721068605440/hecate-offerings

Underworld gods & goddesses. (n.d.). Theoi.com. https://www.theoi.com/greek-mythology/underworld-gods.html

Victory, F. (n.d.). The mythical journey of Oya: An exploration of African mythology. Oriire.com. https://www.oriire.com/article/the-mythical-journey-of-oya-an-exploration-of-african-mythology

Villines, Z. (2022, August 30). What is shadow work? Benefits and exercises. Medicalnewstoday.com. https://www.medicalnewstoday.com/articles/what-is-shadow-work

White Moon Gallery - Sekhmet. (n.d.). https://orderwhitemoon.org/goddess/sekhmet/Sekhmet2.html

Who Is The Norse Equivalent Of Persephone? (2023, October 14). Viking Style. https://viking.style/who-is-the-norse-equivalent-of-persephone/

Wigington, P. (2019, September 17). Introduction to Slavic Mythology. ThoughtCo. https://www.thoughtco.com/slavic-mythology-4768524

Wiki, C. T. F. (n.d.). Baba Yaga. Fairytale Wiki. https://fairytale.fandom.com/wiki/Baba_Yaga

Willemain-Green, C. (2020, April 9). Inanna's Descent: How We Embrace the Shadow and Integrate Our Wholeness. Earth Daughters. https://www.earthdaughters.org/library/innana-goddess

Willemain-Green, C. (2020, March 22). Lilith the Original Woman: Reclaiming the Wild Instinctual Nature of Woman. Earth Daughters. https://www.earthdaughters.org/library/lilith-goddess

Witchery. (2008, February 11). Goddess Candle Colors. Witchery. https://witchery.wordpress.com/2008/02/11/goddess-candle-colors/

Yap, S. S. (2022, November 9). How to Use the Hecate's Wheel Symbol. Blessed Be Magick. https://blessedbemagick.com/blogs/news/how-to-use-the-hecates-wheel-symbol

Yewá: Orisha of purity and chastity in Santeria. (2021, October 18). Oshaeifa.com. https://en.oshaeifa.com/orisha/yewa/

Zhelyazkov, Y. (2023, June 29). Macha: Celtic goddess of power, fertility, and war. Symbol Sage. https://symbolsage.com/macha-irish-goddess/

Made in the USA
Las Vegas, NV
15 November 2024

11889127R00095